he

Joyce Plotnikoff and Richard Woolfson are independent consultants specialising in civil and criminal justice system projects. Much of their work involves children and the law. They are the authors of 'Timetabling of Interim Care Orders Study' (1994) Department of Health and 'Prosecuting Child Abuse' (1995) Blackstone Press Limited. Joyce Plotnikoff has an English law degree and CQSW and is a member of the Bar of the United States Supreme Court. She is a guardian ad litem and was coordinator of the Child Witness Pack (1993) NSPCC/Childline. Richard Woolfson is a doctor of mathematics and management consultant.

REPORTING TO COURT UNDER THE CHILDREN ACT: A HANDBOOK FOR SOCIAL SERVICES

CORRECTIONS

Regrettably two legal errors have been identified in the text of 'Reporting to Court'. Please bring these to the attention of persons who have already received a copy.

EMERGENCY PROTECTION ORDERS

A child who is the subject of a section 44 emergency protection order is not 'in care' under the 'definitions' section of the Act (section 105). The local authority cannot therefore refuse contact under section 34(6) as this applies only to children in care.

The final three sentences at the foot of page 26 should therefore be replaced by the following:

"The court may give directions in respect of contact which is, or is not, to be allowed between the child and any named person (section 44(6)(a)). These directions may impose conditions (section 44(8)). Subject to any such directions, the authority must allow reasonable contact with persons specified in section 44(13)."

SECURE ACCOMMODATION

Section 25 is the basis of all secure accommodation applications. The first margin note on page 34 should therefore read:

"(NB: This section of the Handbook does not apply to applications in the Youth Court during criminal proceedings)."

June 1996

The Handbook was published by HMSO in January 1996, priced £9.95.

© Crown Copyright 1996

Applications for reproduction should be
made to HMSO Copyright Unit, Norwich NR3 1PD

ISBN 011 321 968 7

Preface

I was delighted to be asked to write this Preface because of what I believe to be the importance of the work that follows it. My real qualification for doing so is experience based on the thousands of pages of reports which I must have read in twenty years' practice in the field of child care as a barrister and latterly as a Circuit Judge.

Over the last few years there has been a significant change in the practice of the civil courts. The traditional dependence on oral evidence has been replaced by an increasing emphasis on setting out cases in writing with consequent curbs on such evidence. Alongside that has gone a new level of scrutiny of local authority plans and the giving of much greater importance to the maintenance of contact between children and their natural families. All this requires early and careful thought by social work practitioners.

Giving evidence or writing a report for court is a specialist skill that is not acquired merely through general social work experience. These reports are not primarily for fellow child care professionals but for magistrates, judges, advocates and their clients. They require both care and proper time for preparation. Courts pre-read reports and the cogent, succinct and obviously well thought out report is not only a great asset but also inspires confidence in the writer. It is always sad when a long, rambling report has the effect of not just concealing but actually undermining what was in fact sound professional practice on the ground.

Hence my warm welcome for this Handbook. The Department of Health has done a signal service in initiating this project and the consultants have provided what I believe will prove a resource of high quality and practical usefulness. The skill and knowledge of the Reference Group, together with others who have kindly assisted, has ensured rigorous scrutiny of the material. Moreover, it has been tried in practice and revised in the light of experience.

This is a Handbook for daily use, not an impressive volume for bookcase decoration. It is written with the needs of the busy (and even nervous) practitioner in mind. Its style and layout makes it easy to use and its scope is sufficient for all practical purposes. I commend it enthusiastically to all social workers who share in the vital work of promoting the welfare of children through the civil justice system.

His Honour Judge Mark Hedley

Acknowledgements

Many people gave freely of their time and experience during the production of the Handbook. Special thanks are due to Wendy Rose, Assistant Chief Inspector, who had overall responsibility for the project and to Arran Poyser, Social Services Inspector, for shepherding the project to completion and chairing the project's Reference Group. Its members included:

Chris Bazell, Clerk to the Justices, Banbury and Bicester Magistrates' Courts
Keith Bilton, Chair, Children and Families Subcommittee, British Association of Social Workers
Clare Bridges, Deputy Clerk to the Justices, Croydon Magistrates' Court
Collette Curran, social worker/ therapist, NSPCC
Rose Dagoo, guardian ad litem and social work consultant
Ann Haig, project leader, Barnardos Counselling Services and guardian ad litem
Ann Mair, Chair, Family Proceedings Committee, Magistrates' Association
Caroline Rowe, Probation Service Division, Home Office
Annie Shepperd, Assistant Director, Children and Families, Sutton Social Services Department
Philip Thomson, Head of Legal Services, Essex County Council
Myra White, Civil and Family Business Branch, Court Service
Trish White, Social Services Inspector, Welsh Office.

Mr Justice Wall and His Honour Judge Hedley provided comments on the draft and Judge Hedley kindly agreed to write the Preface to the Handbook.

Southwark Council participated in a four month field test of the draft Handbook which resulted in substantial revisions. We are indebted to Anne Chan, Assistant Director, Children's Services and Gloria McFarlane, Acting Head of Legal Services for their cooperation, and to all the members of their staff who provided constructive criticism. Feedback was also provided by lawyers and others in the court process who read Social Services' statements which had been written with reference to the Handbook. The evaluation was facilitated by Elizabeth Thompson, senior chief clerk, Inner London Family Proceedings Courts; Ruth Ewen, principal clerk, Children Branch, Principal Registry Family Division; and Anna Faulkner, panel manager, Inner and North London Panel of Guardians ad Litem.

Legal citations were checked by Nicola Harrington, Legal Services Division, Essex County Council. Advice on other aspects of the Handbook was provided by:

Jeremy Barley, solicitor, Ronald Prior and Co. Walthamstow, London
(Association of Lawyers for Children)
Sarah Borthwick, trainer consultant, British Agencies for Adoption
and Fostering
Graham Cole, senior solicitor, Bedfordshire Legal Services
Jacqueline Drennan, foster carer, Bedfordshire
Janice Edgington, assistant lawyer, Legal Services, Lewisham Legal
Services
Philippa Evans, senior principal solicitor, Coventry (Law Society
Child Care Law Joint Liaison Group)
Fiona Ledden, assistant solicitor, Sutton Legal Services (Association
of Lawyers for Children)
Ann Molloy, principal solicitor, Child Care Business Unit, Liverpool
Legal Services (Law Society Child Care Law Joint Liaison Group)
Geoff Orton, National Foster Care Association
Alberta Owusu, principal solicitor, Barnet Legal Services
Peter Riches, Director, LBTC: Training For Care
Paddy Sheehy, guardian ad litem
Ann Stevens, assistant solicitor, Sutton Legal Services
Geoff Wild, solicitor, Kent Legal Services
Val Wykes, Children and Families Team, Westminster Social Services
Department

In the Department of Health, thanks are due to Jim Brown for his
indispensable administrative support, and to Marianne Harper for help
with the design and publication.

We would like to acknowledge our debt to the following primary
sources which we found both thorough and accessible:

Adcock M., White R. and Hollows A. Significant Harm: its
management and outcome (1991) Significant Publications.
Brayne H. and Martin G. Law for Social Workers (1990) Blackstone
Press Ltd. 3rd edition.
National Standards for Probation Service Family Court Work (1994)
Home Office.
Pizzey S. and Davis S. A Guide for Guardians ad Litem in Public
Law Proceedings under the Children Act 1989 (1995) HMSO.
Ryan M. The Children Act 1989 - Putting it into Practice (1994)
Family Rights Group, Arena.
Timms J. Children's Representation - a practitioner's guide (1995)
Sweet and Maxwell.

Illustrations were provided by children from Craigholme School and
Hutchesons' School, Glasgow and Preston Primary School,
Hertfordshire.

Contents

List of figures

−1− | # Introduction

This Handbook aims to help you improve the quality of your written submissions in Children Act proceedings.

Why strive for high standards in reporting to court?

- to promote the best interests of the child
- to provide accurate, accessible and relevant information
- to provide a sound foundation for the action being requested from the court
- because well structured and clearly presented written material is the best preparation for giving oral evidence
- because all written material submitted to the court is automatically disclosed to all the parties before a hearing.

This chapter tells you about the scope of the Handbook and how to use it.

Who is the Handbook for?

The guidance is primarily intended for use within the social services network, for example by:

- practitioners working directly with children and their families
- those managing and supervising this work
- service providers involved in the development of care plans
- family centre staff
- residential workers
- trainers.

Parts of the Handbook should also prove useful to foster carers and professionals in health and education when preparing their statements for court.

The Handbook is not intended to replace advice from the local authority legal adviser.

| **What does the Handbook cover?** | The Handbook relates to public and private law applications under the Children Act 1989. Care proceedings are an example of public law which regulates the intervention of the local authority in parental care of children. Divorce proceedings are an example of private law covering disputes between individuals. |

The Handbook does not cover adoption proceedings, the Human Fertilisation and Embryology Act 1990[1], criminal proceedings[2], or reports prepared by guardians ad litem[3] or probation officers[4].

Public law statements and private law reports

When you provide a statement in public law proceedings, it constitutes evidence on behalf of the local authority. 'Evidence' is any material placed before the court to persuade it of the truth or probability of some fact.

When you submit a report in a private law matter, the facts contained in the report may be treated as evidence and you may be cross-examined on them.

The Children Act requires us to develop new approaches to written submissions to the court. Witness statements have been described as a sensible innovation aimed at a "cards on the table" approach[5]. However, preparation and writing are difficult activities, particularly when they are conducted under pressure of time and competing work demands.

The court perspective

The court will welcome statements which help it to determine findings of fact and reasons for its decisions. In its inquisitorial role the court may ask questions which probe the issues and test the evidence. These tasks are made more difficult if magistrates and judges have to sift through lengthy statements and reports in order to identify what is relevant. In some cases, they have described documents as:

- insufficiently focused
- failing to distinguish between fact and opinion
- reproducing large parts of case records with little editing or structure
- failing to discuss the best interests of the child.

Coordinate local authority statement

Local authority statements in the same case are often repetitious. This can be avoided by consultation between authors and the legal adviser to ensure appropriate cross-referencing.

Written material is disclosed to all parties

The Children Act places a new emphasis on the disclosure of written submissions before a case is heard. To give everyone the chance to prepare their case, all parties are now required to file witness statements from persons whose evidence they intend to call. These statements need to contain the substance of the oral evidence that the party intends to put before the court. Reports are disclosed in the same way.

Include all relevant facts, not only those that support your case

When preparing a statement, you are expected to take an accurate and balanced view of the local authority case. You must expose all relevant facts to examination, whether or not they support the authority's application, and set out the reasons for the order(s) applied for by the authority.

> **It is sometimes difficult to identify what may be relevant to other parties; when in doubt, always consult your legal adviser.**

Local authorities have a very high degree of responsibility for disclosure, and have been criticised by courts for omitting relevant information from statements. The authority cannot omit something just because it may be prejudicial to its own performance or to the outcome it is seeking.

How is the Handbook organised?

To help you structure the task of drafting statements and reports for court, this Handbook offers:

- step-by-step advice
- examples
- checklists.

Materials in the Handbook should be adapted to your needs and experience as well as to local requirements.

The Handbook provides suggestions for good practice, not a prescription for the 'definitive' statement or report.

Equally, the checklists are not exhaustive and you may wish to add your own notes. Where there are specific requirements for what *must* be included in your statement, this is made clear in the text.

The Handbook breaks down the drafting of written evidence into its component parts. The chapters following this introduction are grouped into five categories, differentiated by coloured blocks on page edges:

- chapters two to five assist in preparation, timetabling and liaison with others in the court process
- chapters six and seven describe the requirements of specific public and private law applications
- chapters eight to thirteen address the content of your statement or report
- chapters fourteen and fifteen cover the local authority's contact and care plans
- chapter sixteen contains guidance on giving evidence at court.

Figure 5 on page 52, *Selecting what should go into your statement*, cross-references categories of information, Children Act sections and Handbook chapters.

Throughout the Handbook, the term 'case conference' includes, where appropriate, child protection conferences.

The Annex provides a checklist to assist foster carers in planning the content of their statements prior to discussion with the local authority legal adviser.

Summaries of Children Act sections have been included in the text. When writing reports or statements, always check the Act itself and subsequent amendments. Discuss questions of interpretation with your local authority legal adviser. Case law cited in the Handbook is current as of September 1995.

Figure 1: Guiding principles in the Children Act

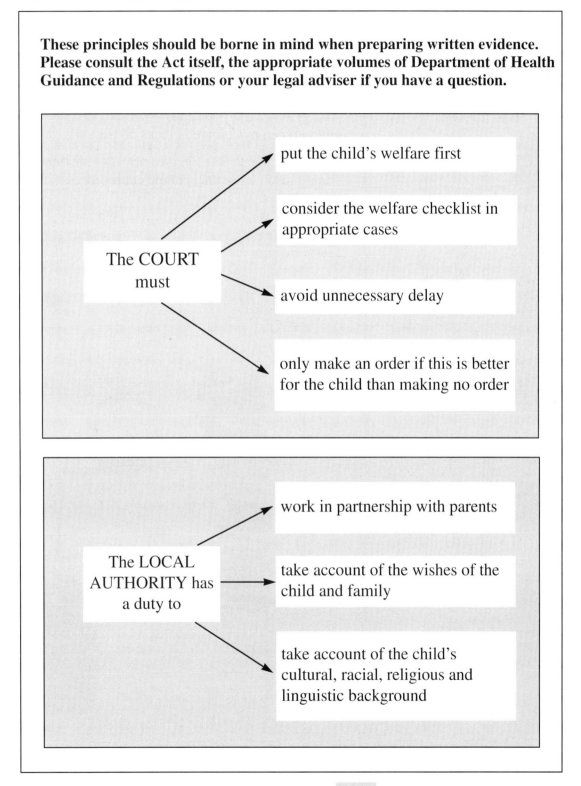

These principles should be borne in mind when preparing written evidence. Please consult the Act itself, the appropriate volumes of Department of Health Guidance and Regulations or your legal adviser if you have a question.

The COURT must

put the child's welfare first

consider the welfare checklist in appropriate cases

avoid unnecessary delay

only make an order if this is better for the child than making no order

The LOCAL AUTHORITY has a duty to

work in partnership with parents

take account of the wishes of the child and family

take account of the child's cultural, racial, religious and linguistic background

1 Local Authority Circular 94(15); Human Fertilisation and Embryology Authority (1993) Code of Practice. Available from 0171 377 5077 (revised Code in preparation).

2 NACRO (1993) Criminal Justice Act 1991. Pre-Sentence Reports - A Handbook for Probation Officers and Social Workers. National Association for the Care and Resettlement of Offenders.

3 Timms J. (1991) Manual of Practice for Guardians ad Litem and Reporting Officers. HMSO; Pizzey S. and Davis J. (1995) A Guide for Guardians ad Litem in Public Law Proceedings under the Children Act 1989. HMSO.

4 Home Office (1994) National Standards for Probation Service Family Court Welfare Work.

5 The Right Honourable the Lord Woolf (1995). Access to Justice: Interim report to the Lord Chancellor on the civil justice system in England and Wales, section 3.9.

Reading the files
Gillian (14)

–2–

Preparation

You are more likely to produce a well-organised and focused statement for court if you spend some time organising your thoughts and the materials first. The early development of a case chronology is particularly useful (see chapter twelve). This chapter suggests some other ideas to assist in preparation.

Identify key issues

The court does not know the background to your case. What is the purpose of the local authority application? Suppose you have to explain this orally. Take a few minutes to jot down the key issues, for example:

- what has happened?
- why is an order needed and what would be its purpose?
- why now?
- is an expert assessment needed (see chapter five)?

Read the records

Some of the events that led to the application for a court order may pre-date the involvement of the current social worker.

It is essential to read the whole file, not just transfer summaries. Previous files relating to the child or family should be retrieved and read.

Reading and note-taking are time-consuming and need to be scheduled into your personal timetable as described in chapter three.

Make lists

You may wish to sketch out:

- a family tree, including the wider family (the court is likely to find this useful)
- the family's history of involvement with social services (the reasons why this was initiated and by whom, frequency of interactions, services offered/ provided, placements etc.)
- the family's involvement with other agencies, for example health, education, housing and child guidance

- the child's record on the child protection register
- the history of case conferences, planning meetings and decision-making.

Summarise your own involvement with the child and family, including:

- the length of such involvement (and, if recent, the steps taken to familiarise yourself with the case)
- the number of contacts with individual members
- whether home visits were by appointment or unscheduled
- details of and reasons for appointments missed by family members or yourself.

Consider whether there are any documents on file which should be attached to your statement as an annex, for example:

- a contract or agreement with the family
- an assessment report
- a letter from the child or parent
- a letter from the social worker to the family.

Citing research

Citing research should be the exception rather than the rule. If you wish to refer to the theoretical basis for your opinion, be prepared to identify the author of the cited research and the name of the publication in which it appeared. It is often preferable to refer to articles or books which provide an overview of findings on a particular subject, making you less susceptible to challenge on the basis that you have singled out research which supports the local authority's position. Be aware of research which came to a different conclusion. You may be asked about such findings in cross-examination. If you are in any doubt about the advisability of research references, consult your legal adviser.

Verify where possible

Are there any steps you should take to verify information for the court case? For example, where school absenteeism is an issue, have you asked the education welfare officer for a certificate of attendance?

Explain the reasons for the application

When the local authority decides to make an application for a court order, you should:

- consult the child and other relevant people
- explain why the local authority considers it necessary to make the application
- ensure that the parents understand the contents and purpose of court documents if they have not yet instructed a solicitor
- provide those with parental responsibility with a list of solicitors on the Law Society Children Panel and a copy of 'The Children Act and the Courts - A Guide for Parents'[1].

The way in which this consultation process was carried out and the responses of the child, family and others to the local authority action should be described in the local authority's evidence.

Be aware of special needs

Appropriate provision should be made for a child or parent with communication difficulties[2], including language and literacy problems. Sensorily impaired children and adults may need information to be provided in a specific format. For the blind or visually impaired this could be braille, tape or large print. The deaf and hard of hearing have a range of communication needs depending on the type and age of onset of their hearing impairment.

When applying for an order, you should advise the court in an annex to the application of the child or party's special needs. Your statement should describe the method(s) of communication employed.

---

1   Available from Department of Health Distribution Centre, PO Box 410, Wetherby LS23 7LN; telephone 01937 840250, fax 01937 845381.
2   Department of Health (1991) The Children Act 1989 Guidance and Regulations Volume 3, Family Placements para. 2.71. HMSO.

–3–

Timetabling at court and within the local authority

> The Children Act emphasises the need to avoid delay and requires the court to set a timetable that brings the case to a conclusion as quickly as possible in the best interests of the child. The timetable must allow for adequate preparation by participants but the scheduling of events should maintain a sense of urgency.
>
> This chapter:
>
> - identifies ways in which social services can contribute to the court timetable
> - suggests how you can manage and timetable the preparation of your written statement or report for court.

Timetabling at court

Delay is likely to be prejudicial

> SECTION 1(2)
>
> **Delay in deciding any question about the child's upbringing is likely to prejudice the child's welfare.**

The Act recognises that, in general, the child's welfare is likely to suffer as a consequence of delay in proceedings. The court must set a timetable for any case involving children and issue directions to ensure the case is heard as quickly as possible (sections 11(1) and 32(1)).

'Avoidable' delay

You should discuss with your legal adviser:

- the effect of delay on the child in question
- whether the timetable is prejudicial to the child's interests
- the availability of an expert witness on behalf of the local authority.

10

> **Your statement should address the tension between the 'no delay' priciple and the importance of assessing the child's needs.**

Provide time estimates

Before the directions appointment (see below), it is your responsibility to provide your legal adviser with an estimate of the time required to prepare your written evidence and the reasons, taking account of the consultation involved in developing the care plan. You should also indicate your availability for court hearings. Providing this information in advance will assist your legal adviser in contributing to the court timetable.

The maximum time that the court is likely to allow for filing any one statement is 28 days. Typically, the court requires statements and reports to be filed in a logical sequence. This allows subsequent statements to comment on those which were filed earlier. In public law cases, the local authority usually files the first statement, though it may also file later evidence. The report of the guardian ad litem (where one is appointed) is always the last scheduled submission. Court rules require that it is filed seven days[1] before the final hearing unless otherwise ordered.

Notify legal adviser of potential delays

> **When a timetabled statement is filed late, time for response by other parties is reduced and their statements are likely to be delayed. Opportunities for pre-hearing negotiation (one of the goals of the open exchange of evidence) may be curtailed.**

You must comply with the court timetable to the best of your ability and submit your statement to the legal adviser in good time. It is the adviser's duty to ensure that documents are filed with the court and served on all parties. The court has powers to impose a wasted costs order as a penalty on the party responsible[2] and to determine that the late statement should not be admitted.

If there is a possibility that your statement will not be ready on time or you become aware that any other local authority evidence may be late (such as the report from an assessment), let your legal adviser know immediately. It is important that significant departures from the timetable be brought to the court's attention as a further directions appointment may be needed.

'Purposeful' delay

In certain circumstances, the need to hold a final hearing as quickly as possible may be outweighed by other factors. Delay is 'purposeful' when specific activities are scheduled, with positive reasons for prolonging matters in the long-term interests of the child, for example a focused assessment, trial home stays or any other reasonable attempt at rehabilitation.

If a particular course of action proposed by the local authority will extend the proceedings, specify the amount of time required and explain why this delay is in the child's best interests.

Directions appointments

The court controls the progress of the case by issuing directions and an agreed timetable for filing parties' evidence with the court. Directions may be issued at a court hearing or at a directions appointment chaired by a court clerk.

At a directions appointment, the following matters can be addressed[3]:

- the setting of a timetable for the filing and service of witness statements and documents
- the setting of dates for a subsequent directions appointment and hearings
- the appointment of a guardian ad litem for the child
- persons to be joined as parties
- the attendance of the child at court
- the submission of evidence including expert reports
- the preparation of welfare reports under section 7
- transfer to another court or consolidation with other proceedings concerning the same family
- applications for interim orders
- other matters that the court considers appropriate.

Personal plan for court work

Timetabling within the local authority

The local authority witness should develop a personal timetable running alongside that of the court. This plan should include the scheduling of:

- dates on which your statements are due to be filed with the court
- time for reading files, preparation and writing
- time for typing and review
- time for copying and distribution
- dates on which you are required to attend court
- consultation contributing to formulation of the care plan
- decision-making meetings (include booking the room and sending invitations)
- discussions with the guardian ad litem
- appointments with your legal adviser, including consultation prior to the final hearing.

The manager's responsibilities

The local authority manager has a responsibility to:

- give priority to court work being undertaken by staff
- record the personal timetable of social worker witnesses on a unit-wide basis, so that the manager is aware of all team commitments to court work
- ensure that the witness has adequate time to prepare and write statements
- monitor compliance with the court timetable
- ensure that the care plan is based on a realistic allocation of resources
- review critically statements and reports.

1   Rule 11(7), Family Proceedings Courts (Children Act 1989) Rules 1991; rule 4.11(7), Family Proceedings Rules 1991.

2   R v Nottingham County Council [1993] 1 FCR 576.

3   Rule 14(2), Family Proceedings Courts (Children Act 1989) Rules 1991; rule 4.14(2), Family Proceedings Rules 1991.

–4– The local authority legal adviser

Arrangements for the delivery of legal services vary among local authorities. Child protection work may be:

- handled 'in house' by a local authority lawyer
- assigned on an individual case basis to specialist solicitors in private practice
- contracted out by competitive tender.

Increasingly, lawyers handling this work have to account for their time in a way which has resource implications for the social services department. You should be aware of the arrangements for delivery of legal services in your area.

In individual cases, the legal adviser may brief a barrister to represent the local authority at court. Responsibility for day-to-day management of the case remains with the legal adviser.

Source of independent legal advice

The local authority legal adviser works closely with social services and other agencies involved in child protection. The adviser acts on the instructions of the social services department and should always be consulted before proceedings are begun.

Legal adviser's duties

The legal adviser's primary duties are to the court and the interests of the child. The adviser's client is the local authority but the day-to-day working relationship is with the Director of Social Services, acting through local managers and social workers.

Certain common principles apply, irrespective of local provisions for legal services. It is the responsibility of the legal adviser to:

- maintain the integrity of the local authority before the court
- examine the local authority's case at an early stage

- attend case conferences and formal planning meetings whenever possible
- ensure that all relevant information is before the court and the other parties
- ensure that the statement represents the witness's evidence as accurately as possible and that the witness understands and signs every page[1]
- meet strict timetable requirements.

The local authority should be an equal participant in informed discussions about the court timetable. On occasion, the local authority's requirements are not taken fully into consideration by the court because of the inadequacy of the information presented. The local authority legal adviser should:

- provide witness availability dates
- consult with those involved to provide time estimates for the submission of statements, expert reports, the chronology and the care plan
- consult with the other parties about the timetable well in advance of a directions hearing
- develop a draft timetable for consideration by the court.

In exceptional circumstances, the legal adviser's duties to the court and the interests of the child transcend those to social services and the client authority. For example, any instructions from social services that documentation or information relevant to the case should not be disclosed is likely to be challenged by the legal adviser.

Resolving disputes

In the unlikely event of a dispute arising between the social services department and the legal adviser concerning disclosure or the management of the case, the issue should be addressed at a senior level in both organisations.

Document bundles

Court guidelines have been issued[2] regarding legal representatives' preparation of document bundles. Social workers should be aware of the legal adviser's responsibilities with respect to indexing, pagination etc. and the time requirements for bundle preparation.

Figure 2: Court structure for proceedings under the Children Act 1989

HOUSE OF LORDS

- Appeals from Court of Appeal

COURT OF APPEAL (Civil Division)

- Appeals from High Court and county court

HIGH COURT (Family Division)

- Public and private law cases involving complex points or issues of law
- Private law applications made by children
- Applications when there are pending proceedings, or to vary, extend or discharge existing orders of the court
- Applications under CA1989 from family proceedings court
- Inherent jurisdiction

COUNTY COURT

Care Centre
Circuit Judge
- Transferred public law cases
- Applications when there are pending proceedings, or to vary, extend or discharge existing orders of the court
- Private law cases

District Judge
- Directions in public and private law cases
- Transfer applications refused by family proceedings court referred for reconsideration
- Powers to make certain preliminary or limited and agreed orders in public and private law cases

Family Hearing Centre
Circuit Judge
- Private law cases

District Judge
- Directions in private law cases
- Powers to make preliminary and agreed orders in private law cases

FAMILY PROCEEDINGS COURT

- Most public law cases are commenced here
- Private law cases may be commenced here

Reproduced with kind permission from Pizzey S. and Davis J.(1995) A Guide for Guardians ad Litem in Public Law Proceedings under the Children Act 1989. Department of Health. HMSO.

1   Children Act Advisory Committee Annual Report 1993/4
     p. 23.
2   B v B (Practice Judgment) [1994] 1 FCR 805.

–5–

Working with experts and other key participants

This chapter describes the responsibilities of the local authority:

- to provide information to assist the court when an assessment or expert examination is under consideration
- to liaise with other participants in the court process, namely:

      the guardian ad litem
      the interpreter
      the Official Solicitor.

Referral for assessment or expert examination

Is an expert necessary?

It is essential that the parties and the court are clear about the purpose of an assessment, how it will serve the best interests of the child and in what way it will add to already available evidence. Is the assessment necessary to resolve issues about the threshold conditions or the care plan? What aspects of these require an expert opinion? Lack of confidence in social work evidence can lead to the commissioning of expert reports which confirm the authority's earlier submissions. This can contribute to delays in reaching final hearings.

Pre-hearing enquiries

Once the application has been made, the child cannot be medically or psychiatrically examined or otherwise assessed for the purpose of preparing expert evidence without leave of the court[1]. If the child is of sufficient understanding, he or she is entitled to refuse such an examination.

Where the local authority wishes to refer the child, family or both for assessment, before this matter is raised at a court hearing the authority should enquire about the availability of those who might carry out the assessment. Consultations should also be held with the other parties, particularly the guardian ad litem who advises the court on this issue.

The local authority should tell the court[2]:

- the issues to be addressed in the assessment
- why allowing time for the assessment or examination is in the best interests of the child
- the category of expert evidence in question
- its relevance to the welfare of the child and the issues to be decided in the case
- the name and qualifications of the individual expert or organisation proposed to conduct the assessment
- the time needed to carry out the assessment
- dates to avoid for the expert in scheduling the hearing
- the views of the other parties.

The Children Act Advisory Committee has recommended the use of a core curriculum vitae for an expert witness[3].

The referral letter

The letter instructing the expert should specify the issues to be addressed in the report. These might include:

- the factual basis for the local authority application
- family histories which may be relevant to current concerns
- the care plan, including the possibility of rehabilitation
- contact
- which orders, if any, are appropriate.

Joint referral preferable

Every effort should be made to secure agreement:

'to a single programme of examination or assessment, which could if necessary be observed by, or conducted jointly with, a medical practitioner nominated by the parents... *The court will expect to be advised on these matters by the guardian ad litem...* In the last resort and where there is a conflict of views between the parties (the parents, the applicant and the guardian ad litem) the court must determine the type of assessment to be carried out and by whom based on the nature of the concern and what is in the best interests of the child'[4] (emphasis added).

When parties consent to a joint referral, the letter of instruction should be circulated for agreement and the statements and other documents to be disclosed to the expert should be listed. The referral letter must be attached to the expert's report or assessment when it is filed with the court. Consent to a joint referral does not invariably involve sharing the cost of the assessment, which should be addressed separately.

The timetable

The court should be asked:

- to specify the matters to be addressed in the expert's report
- for authority to disclose relevant papers to the expert
- to fix the date when the report of the assessment is to be filed with the court
- to fix a directions appointment immediately after completion of the assessment to reassess the case, decide what further evidence is required (expert and otherwise) and obtain further directions for a speedy hearing
- to fix a date for the final hearing.

Timeliness of expert reports

Late filing of expert reports and assessments is a significant cause of delay, often requiring final hearings to be rescheduled.

> **The referral letter should emphasise the importance of filing the report in accordance with the timetable. The author should be requested to notify the appropriate legal adviser at the earliest opportunity if the report is likely to be late. It is not acceptable for the expert to give such notice on or just before the due date.**

The court has the power to impose a wasted costs order if late reports cause an adjournment[5].

Informing the child and family of the outcome

The conclusions of the expert report or assessment may be deeply distressing to the child and family. The letter of instruction should clarify who has responsibility for informing the child and family of the outcome of the assessment.

Example of an excerpt from a commissioning letter to a psychologist:

'Towards the close of your psychological assessment, it would be most helpful if you would allow time to discuss your conclusion and recommendations with Mr and Mrs Taylor and, if appropriate, with Simone (aged 9) and to incorporate their responses into your report. If they have not been informed of your conclusion and recommendations, please make this clear in your report to the court.'

Keeping the expert up-to-date

It should be established among the parties who has responsibility to supply all statements filed with the court (including the care plan) to the expert who may be asked to comment on them while giving evidence.

Liaison with other participants

The social worker may have contact with other key individuals involved in the court process:

- the guardian ad litem
- the interpreter
- the Official Solicitor.

You should be aware of their duties and any responsibilities you have in assisting them to carry out their role.

The guardian ad litem

In public law cases, the child's interests are usually represented by a guardian *ad litem* ('in the proceedings'), appointed by the court at an early stage. Most guardians are social workers who are members of local panels. They are not employed by the local authority making the application.

The guardian's duties

It is the guardian's responsibility[6] to:

- safeguard and promote the welfare of the child
- ensure that the child's views are made known to the court.

To fulfill this role, the guardian:

- appoints a solicitor to act for the child (unless one is already appointed by the court)

21

- gives advice to the child in a way the child can understand
- discusses the issues with all the parties before the case is heard
- gathers evidence
- provides the court with an impartial written report recommending what is best for the child.

The guardian advises the court about:

- the timetable
- the appointment of an expert
- whether anyone else who would be likely to safeguard the interests of the child should be involved in the proceedings
- whether the child is of sufficient understanding to refuse medical or psychiatric examination or other assessment
- the wishes of the child
- the appropriate forum for the proceedings
- any other relevant matter.

Attendance at meetings

Local authorities and panels of guardians ad litem usually have a local policy on the invitation of guardians to planning meetings and case conferences. Where family members are present the guardian usually attends only as an observer and may withdraw during decision-making and when legal advice is given.

Full access to records

Section 42 authorises the guardian to examine and take copies of local authority records concerning the child who is the subject of the application. This includes minutes of case conferences, planning meetings and documents relating to any potential adoption or adopters. Social workers and guardians should be aware that if a guardian takes a copy of a record and refers to it in the report, the record can become evidence and copies may need to be provided to other parties.

The guardian's report is submitted to the court in accordance with directions but usually at least seven days before the final hearing. The guardian has a responsibility to comment on the local authority care plan and this should be provided to the guardian as soon as it is available.

The timing of chronology preparation (see chapter twelve) should be discussed with the guardian. If the local authority's chronology is made available to the guardian at an early stage, it is likely to avoid duplication of effort.

Avoiding duplication of appointments

Pending court proceedings create a lot of extra pressure for children, families and foster carers. Many additional activities may be involved such as assessment appointments and supervised contact sessions. It is helpful if social workers and guardians notify one another of their appointments with children and families so that scheduling conflicts can be avoided.

The interpreter[7]

Interpreter must be impartial

When you do not speak the language of the child or of any party and their full participation would not otherwise be possible, an interpreter must be used in interviews. It is essential that an interpreter remains impartial and professional and has an understanding of welfare or legal work. The use of family members, particularly children, is inappropriate. Find an interpreter who speaks the family's mother tongue rather than a language or dialect in which they can 'get by'.

Give the interpreter sufficient information about the assignment, including the terminology, concepts and procedures involved, to allow for preparation.

Allow enough time. During an interpreted interview, everything has to be said twice. Ask the interpreter to speak in the first person when translating. Give full, clear explanations of concepts and procedures. A non-specialist interpreter may not know the precise meaning of some terms and indeed, they may not exist in the same form in the other language.

Interpreters at court

Welsh interpreters are provided and paid for as necessary by courts in Wales. In respect of all other languages, the provision and payment of interpreters in civil proceedings is the responsibility of the party concerned.

Additional time must be allowed for court hearings when interpretation is necessary.

The Official Solicitor

A small proportion of cases involve the Official Solicitor, a lawyer in charge of a department of civil servants, who represents children and also adults with learning difficulties or psychiatric illnesses in court. He will consider acting for a child where[8]:

- there is disputed or conflicting medical evidence (including psychiatric evidence)
- there is a substantial foreign element
- special or exceptional points of law are involved
- the child is already represented by the Official Solicitor.

A member of the Official Solicitor's staff investigates the case and liaison with this person should be conducted as with the guardian ad litem.

Some members of the Official Solicitor's staff are lawyers but few have social work or other child care qualifications. Cases involving the Official Solicitor are usually complex or controversial.

1 Rule 18(1), Family Proceedings Courts (Children Act 1989) Rules 1991; rule 4.18(1), Family Proceedings Rules 1991.

2 Guidance given by Mr Justice Wall, 7 March 1994.

3 Annual Report 1993/94, pp. 24-25.

4 Department of Health (1991) The Children Act 1989 Guidance and Regulations Volume 1, Court Orders para. 3.49. HMSO.

5 R v Nottingham County Council [1993] 1 FCR 576.

6 Rule 11(4), Family Proceedings Courts (Children Act 1989) Rules 1991; rule 4.11(4), Family Proceedings Rules 1991.

7 For information about the National Register of Public Service Interpreters, contact the Nuffield Interpreter Project (telephone 0171 631 0566, fax 0171 323 4877) or the Institute of Linguists (telephone 0171 359 7445, fax 0171 354 0202).

8 The Children Act Advisory Committee Annual Report 1992/93 Annex 3.

Public law applications

This chapter deals with applications for:

- emergency protection orders (section 44)
- child assessment orders (section 43)
- care or supervision orders (section 31)
- discharge and variation of care and supervision orders (section 39)
- secure accommodation orders (section 25).

The power of the court to order an investigation is dealt with in chapter seven. Contact and related issues are covered in chapter thirteen.

Emergency protection orders

SECTION 44

(1) Where any person applies for an emergency protection order, the court may make an order if it is satisfied

    (a) there is reasonable cause to believe that the child is likely to suffer significant harm if
        (i) he is not removed or
        (ii) he does not remain in the place in which he is then being accommodated; or

    (b) in the case of an application made by a local authority
        (i) enquiries about the child are being made under section 47(1)(b); and
        (ii) those enquiries are being frustrated by access to the child being unreasonably refused and that the applicant has reasonable cause to believe that access to the child is required as a matter of urgency.

Purpose	An emergency protection order gives the applicant parental responsibility for the duration of the order. The applicant must exercise that parental responsibility:

- to safeguard and promote the welfare of the child
- where necessary, by removing the child to accommodation provided, or
- by preventing the child's removal from his or her present accommodation.

The court may make directions for contact with the child and medical or psychiatric examination or assessment.

Why is an emergency order necessary?	Wherever possible, legal advice should be obtained before seeking an emergency protection order. Explain to the court why the child's safety is immediately threatened and (if relevant) describe how access to the child has been unreasonably refused. The court will only make an emergency protection order in extremely urgent cases.
Specify significant harm	Describe the significant harm suffered or why it is reasonable to believe that the child is likely to suffer significant harm. If there is a suspected non-accidental injury, a medical report should be obtained. (For further discussion of 'significant harm', see section 31 applications below.)
	You will probably not be able to address all relevant issues in writing. You should be prepared to provide oral evidence to the court.
Describe any consultation	Although the circumstances are likely to require urgent attention, consultation with other professionals who are closely involved will assist in a measured approach. If consultation has taken place, this should be reflected.
Proposed contact to be reasonable	If an emergency protection order is made, the local authority must allow parents reasonable contact with their child through visits and phone calls unless this puts the child's welfare at risk. The local authority may only refuse contact if it is satisfied that the need is urgent and it is necessary to do so in order to safeguard or promote the child's welfare. The refusal cannot last more than seven days (section 34(6)). In order to extend this period it is necessary to apply for an order under section 34(4).

Action following the order

Be prepared to tell the court what steps the local authority intends to take following the making of the order regarding placement, treatment or other aspect of the care plan.

Verify if possible

An application for an emergency protection order can either be made with advance notice or *ex parte*, that is without the presence of the parents or their legal representative. *Ex parte* applications should be made only in the most compelling circumstances and if the situation is considered to require immediate action. This makes it doubly important that the local authority makes every attempt to verify information relied upon in the application and identifies any information not so verified.

Child assessment orders

SECTION 43

(1) On the application of a local authority or authorised person for a child assessment order, the court may make the order if it is satisfied

(a) that the applicant has reasonable cause to suspect that the child is suffering, or is likely to suffer significant harm

(b) an assessment of the state of the child's health or development, or of the way in which he has been treated, is required to enable the applicant to determine whether or not the child is suffering, or is likely to suffer, significant harm; and

(c) it is unlikely that such an assessment will be made, or be satisfactory, in the absence of an order under this section.

The child assessment order enables a medical, psychiatric or social work assessment of the child to be made where significant harm is suspected and the parents have refused to cooperate. It is likely that any application will have been preceded by a section 47 investigation.

The application must be made with advance notice to the parents[1].

27

Tell the court:

- about the authority's investigation into the welfare of the child
- what steps were taken to persuade the parents to cooperate with the investigation
- what kind of assessment is sought (it may be of a medical or psychiatric nature) and the questions to be addressed
- the person or institution that will carry out the assessment
- when the assessment will start, how long it will last and whether the child needs to stay away from home overnight (the court will order this only if absolutely necessary)
- the length of the order sought (the maximum is seven days)
- the child's view (the order does not take away the child's own right to refuse a medical examination, so long as he or she is sufficiently able to understand the situation).

Example of excerpt from an application for a child assessment order:

'Doctor G. Crawford, consultant community physician, will conduct an immediate physical examination of the children at their home if we can see them today. She has suggested that in light of the family history, the court grants permission for a full skeletal survey. If the children appear fit and well we do not propose to carry this out today. However, if there is superficial evidence of injuries, Dr Crawford may feel it is necessary for the children to be examined further at hospital. We therefore request a child assessment order for 36 hours, starting today.'

Are there grounds for an EPO?

The court will not make a child assessment order if it is satisfied that there are grounds for making an emergency protection order.

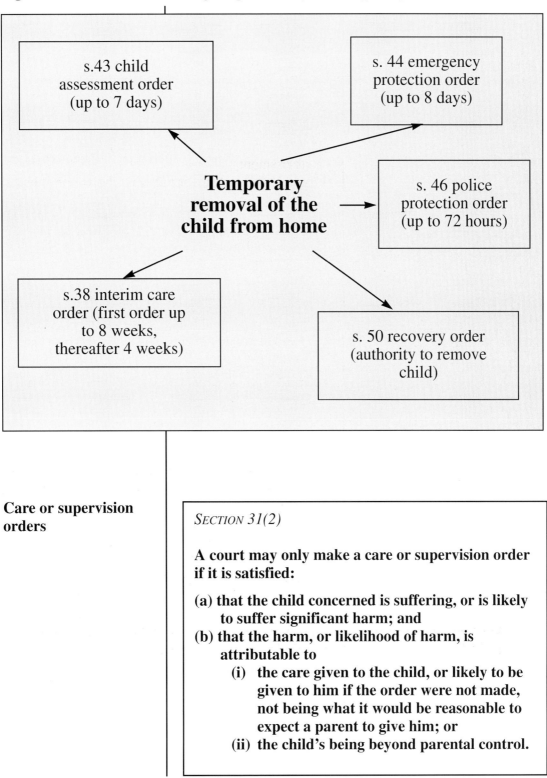

Care or supervision
orders

SECTION 31(2)

A court may only make a care or supervision order
if it is satisfied:

(a) that the child concerned is suffering, or is likely
    to suffer significant harm; and
(b) that the harm, or likelihood of harm, is
    attributable to
    (i) the care given to the child, or likely to be
         given to him if the order were not made,
         not being what it would be reasonable to
         expect a parent to give him; or
    (ii) the child's being beyond parental control.

| The threshold criteria | See the 'Significant Harm Criteria' flow-chart at the end of the discussion of section 31(2). It is important to seek legal advice as to whether the threshold criteria are satisfied. |

The court should be informed about:

- the harm suffered or the reasons for the likelihood of harm, and whether this is attributable to:

    ill-treatment, which may include sexual, physical or emotional abuse <u>or</u>

    the impairment of physical or mental health <u>or</u>

    the impairment of physical, intellectual, emotional or behavioural development

Identify those responsible for causing harm

- the identity of those responsible for causing harm to the child, if known. Where ill-treatment is alleged, this must be proved on the balance of probabilities. Risk arising from past concerns is not enough to satisfy the threshold criteria. The court normally has to consider whether those responsible can be identified

Children with special needs may require a higher standard of parenting care

- the parenting needs of the child in question rather than an average child (a *subjective* test). If the child has particular difficulties this could require a higher standard of care than for the average child[2]

Compare the child's health or development with that of a 'similar' child

- where facts relate to health or development, what could reasonably be expected of a similar child. The standard should only be that which it is reasonable to expect for the child in question, rather than the best that could possibly be achieved (an *objective* test). The court may take account of environmental, social and cultural characteristics[3]

Is the harm 'significant'?

- whether the harm is serious (such as a skull fracture) or is significant because of its implications (for example, a cigarette burn). 'Minor shortcomings in health care or minor deficits in physical, psychological or social development' should not require compulsory intervention unless cumulatively they are having, or are likely to have, serious and lasting effects upon the child[4].

Is the harm attributable to 'care given' or 'likely to be given'?

- how the parent has exercised parental responsibility in the past, and any plans for future care of the child[5]

- the relevant date for the court to determine whether the threshold criteria were satisfied[6].

Example illustrating the issue of relevant dates:

Consider the case of a child who was the subject of an EPO two years ago. On that occasion, the local authority after investigation decided to take no further action. Three months ago, another EPO was obtained by the local authority based on concerns of ill-treatment. Care proceedings were immediately instituted and a number of interim care orders were made. The final hearing is today. The court will look at whether the threshold criteria were satisfied on the date when the more recent EPO was obtained. The court cannot look at the circumstances relating to the EPO two years ago because of the break in child protection procedures. However, if the court decides that the criteria have been satisfied then in deciding what order to make, if any, it will look at the whole history of the case including the EPO incident two years ago.

Distinguish care and supervision orders

The threshold criteria for the making of a care order are the same as those for a supervision order. However, the content of the two orders are completely different and the appropriate choice of order requires an evaluation of future risk. If a supervision order is requested, the role of the authority is limited because parental responsibility is exercised solely by the parent. The authority should describe the details of parental supervision and cooperation on which it relies to safeguard and protect the child[7].

Figure 4: Significant harm criteria

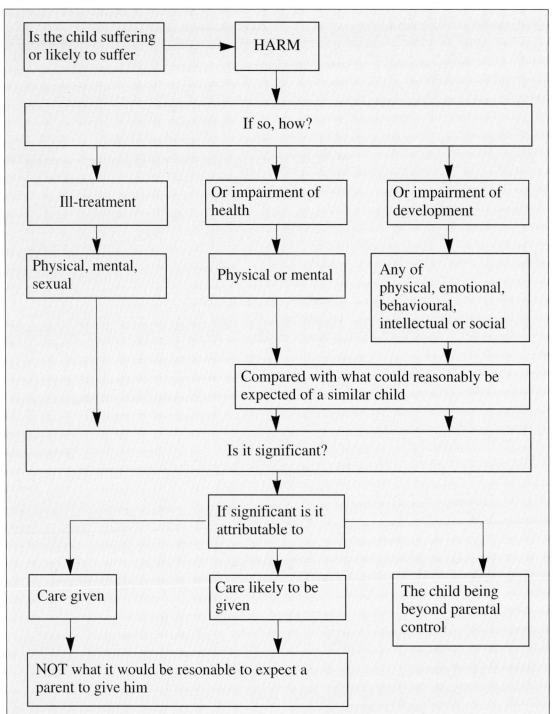

Reproduced with kind permission from Adcock M., White R. and Hollows A. (1991)
Significant Harm: its management and outcome. Significant Publications.

Discharge and variation of care or supervision orders

SECTION 39

(1) A care order may be discharged by the court on the application of any person who has parental responsibility for the child, the child himself, or the local authority designated by the care order.

(2) A supervision order may be discharged by the court on the application of any person who has parental responsibility for the child, the child himself, or the supervisor.

(4) Where a care order is in force, the court may, on application of any person entitled to apply for the order to be discharged, substitute a supervision order for the care order.

When the application is to *discharge* an order, the risk to be considered is that at the date of the discharge hearing. The court will be concerned with evidence of recent harm and assessment of current risk. Except in rare cases, the previous findings of fact in relation to significant harm will be treated as accepted findings, and will not be re-examined[8].

When the application is to vary *a care order to a supervision order*, the previous findings of fact in relation to significant harm will be treated as accepted findings.

When the application is to replace *a supervision order with a care order*, the court has to make a fresh finding on the facts. The court will conduct a full hearing, re-examining the evidence against the criteria in section 31.

Secure accommodation

(NB Section 25 does not apply to applications in the Youth Court during criminal proceedings)

SECTION 25

(1) A child being looked after by the local authority may not be placed or kept in secure accommodation unless it appears:

(a) that
    (i) he has a history of absconding and is likely to abscond from any other description of accommodation and
    (ii) if he absconds, he is likely to suffer significant harm; or

(b) that if he is kept in any other description of accommodation he is likely to injure himself or other persons.

Statutory criteria

A child need not be the subject of a care order before being placed in secure accommodation, but if the parent objects and there is no care order, the child must not be so placed. The maximum length of time during which a child can be kept in secure accommodation before the case must be taken to court is 72 hours in total, whether or not consecutive, in a period of 28 consecutive days. A statement must be produced before the first hearing (a chronology is likely to be particularly useful).

The court must be informed of:

- the child's history of absconding
- the likelihood of absconding from any other type of accommodation
- the likelihood of significant harm to the child if absconding occurs, or
- the grounds for believing that the child is likely to injure himself or other persons if kept in any other type of accommodation.

History of absconding	When considering a child's history of absconding, factors to be considered include:

- whether the child injured himself or others
- any harm that the child suffered while absconding
- the reason for running away
- the child's associates
- over what period the absconding has taken place and with what frequency
- did the child commit any offences
- where the child ran to (did the child remain nearby)
- did the child return voluntarily
- whether the child's behaviour is a reflection of the pattern of the institution (including the frequency and reasons for the absconding of other residents).

Order mandatory if statutory criteria satisfied

If the statutory criteria are satisfied, then it is mandatory for the court to make the order. If the criteria are not satisfied, no order can be made however much the child's welfare may seem to require it.

The wishes and feelings of the child will be taken into account by the court when considering the application even though there is no statutory requirement to do so[9].

Views of child and family

Before making a decision in relation to any child being looked after, the local authority has a general duty to ascertain the child's wishes and feelings and those of the parent, other persons with parental responsibility and any other relevant person (section 22). These should be explored and presented to the court. Consideration should be given to:

- the child's understanding of the purpose of the hearing
- whether the child has been persuaded to agree to secure accommodation and whether this agreement is valid
- whether the child or family has any views as to any form of alternative accommodation that might meet his needs.

The only exception to this general duty to consult is where the local authority exercises its powers for the purpose of protecting members of the public from serious injury (section 22(6)-(8)).

35

Physical and mental health	The local authority should provide information about:

- the child's physical and mental health (section 25(1)(b))
- whether the child's capabilities or understanding are permanently or temporarily impaired by medication, learning difficulty or psychiatric illness
- the ability of local child and adolescent services to assist the child.

Length of order considered separately

The court must consider the length of the order as a separate issue. The authority should state how long it considers the order should last and may refer to the welfare checklist in this context. Upon a first application, a secure accommodation order can be made for a maximum of three months. On a second application, the maximum duration is six months. Instead of making a full order at the first hearing, the court may make a 28 day interim secure order which counts towards the length of the final order. The child's interests are best served if interim and final orders are kept as short as possible.

Describe clearly the objectives of secure accommodation

The court should be informed about:

- the details of the care plan
- the aims to be served by secure accommodation and to what extent restriction of liberty is consistent with the care plan
- how those providing the secure accommodation meet these aims
- to what extent these aims can be achieved within the maximum initial period of the order.

The choice of secure unit

With the needs of the child in mind and in the context of the care plan, the characteristics of the proposed placement should be described. Factors may include:

- the age, gender and race of other residents
- the number being detained for certain grave crimes under section 53 Children and Young Persons Act 1933
- the number of children on remand
- the number of Police and Criminal Evidence Act 1984 detainees
- whether, in the case of placement in a psychiatric hospital, there is sufficient evidence that the child suffers from a psychiatric illness.

Secure accommodation is a last resort

Secure accommodation is not a form of punishment and must not be used as a 'breathing space', because no other placement is available or because the child is being a nuisance. The local authority must:

- demonstrate that all alternatives have been comprehensively considered or pursued and rejected, including a thorough review of local facilities[10]
- describe what other forms of accommodation have been tried
- describe whether alternative forms of accommodation exist.

Children usually become the subject of secure accommodation applications after intervention by various agencies. Describe any process of consultation with others.

1 Rule 4(3), Family Proceedings Courts (Children Act 1989) Rules 1991; rule 4.4(3), Family Proceedings Rules 1991.

2 Adcock M., White R. and Hollows A. (1991) Significant Harm: its management and outcome. Significant Publications p. 9.

3 Department of Health (1991) The Children Act 1989 Guidance and Regulations Volume 1, Court Orders para. 3.20. HMSO.

4 Department of Health (1991) The Children Act 1989 Guidance and Regulations Volume 1, Court Orders para. 3.21. HMSO.

5 Department of Health (1991) The Children Act 1989 Guidance and Regulations Volume 1, Court Orders para. 3.23. HMSO.

6 Re M (a Minor) (Care Order: Threshold Conditions) [1994] 3 All ER 298.

7 Re S (J) (A Minor) (Care or Supervision Order) 1993 2 FLR 919.

8 Re S (Minors); TLR 5 July 1995.

9 Hereford and Worcester County Council v S [1993] 2 FLR 360.

10 The local authority is under a specific duty to avoid the need for children in their area to be placed in secure accommodation (Schedule 2, para. 7(c)).

−7− Private law: court-ordered enquiries

This chapter describes the preparation of reports in response to court-ordered investigations under sections 7 and 37. Although section 37 enquiries can be ordered by the court in public law cases, most originate in private law proceedings.

In private law matters, the court may direct Social Services to provide information concerning the child's welfare, for example where there is a dispute between the parties about the residence of the child, contact or parental responsibility.

When you prepare a report in a private law matter at the request of the court, it does not have the legal status of a witness statement. However, as a matter of good practice, the same standards should be applied to the contents.

Local authority legal advisers are not always notified automatically of requests for reports from the court but you should still consult the adviser if you have any questions.

Welfare reports

SECTION 7

(1) A court considering any question with respect to a child under the Children Act may ask a probation officer, local authority or other appropriate person such as the NSPCC, to report to the court on such matters relating to the welfare of that child as are required to be dealt with in the report.
(3) The report may be made orally or in writing as the court requires.

Purpose of s. 7 enquiry

Section 7 reports may be prepared by probation officers (in practice, family court welfare officers)[1], social workers and the NSPCC. In most cases, the report is prepared by a social worker only where there is current or recent involvement with the family. The general principles of the Children Act apply.

The purpose of a section 7 enquiry is to provide the court with information and advice as to what (if any) orders should be made to promote the child's welfare. This does not mean conducting a full 'orange book assessment'[2]. It is not your role to resolve disputes when preparing a welfare report, though you may identify opportunities for helping the parties to reach agreement.

Scope

A Practice Direction[3] advises courts to specify the nature of the enquiries which they wish the court welfare officer to undertake. The Children Act Committee has provided a Best Practice Note and model referral form for the bench when ordering a welfare report[4]. Nevertheless, section 7 reports are often ordered without clear reasons being given by the court. Even if the court has identified specific areas of concern, you are not prevented from bringing other relevant matters to its attention. Early consideration should be given to the need for expert evidence in such a case.

If you have any question about the scope or nature of the enquiry, you can request further directions from the court. This may not require a hearing as some requests for directions can be dealt with by letter (seek the advice of the local authority legal adviser).

As in other enquiries concerning the best interests of the child, you should advise the parties that your discussions with them are not confidential and may be disclosed in your report. Section 7(4) provides that any matter referred to in the report, whether hearsay or opinion, is admissible so long as it is relevant. Nevertheless, where hearsay evidence is relied upon, this should be made explicit in the report as should the source of the information. The court needs information and advice to make judgements as to the weight to be accorded to hearsay evidence.

Relevant sources

Information may already be held about the child, parties or prospective members of the household in:

- the local authority child protection register
- social work records
- probation records
- police records.

Adult subjects should always be informed if a check is being made and be given an opportunity to comment on the accuracy of any factual information revealed about them. The report should confirm whether this has occurred.

Planning your enquiry

Consider whether it is appropriate to:

- see the parties separately and/ or together
- visit each party at home
- contact other relevant agencies such as the school, doctor and health visitor
- see each child alone and with siblings
- see each child with both parents
- see each child with each parent
- see any other significant carers
- see the new partners of a parent.

Where difficulties occur, discuss them with the court and, if necessary, ask for further directions.

The child's wishes and feelings

> **When conducting a section 7 enquiry, there is a strong presumption that you should see the child. If you do not do so, give your reasons in the report.**

During meetings with the child:

- give the child the opportunity to express wishes and feelings
- do not allow a child to be forced to express a view or to take responsibility for decisions which properly belong to adults.

Parties have a choice

Joint meetings should be encouraged but cannot be compelled. Inform the parties in writing that:

- they are free to choose whether to attend a joint meeting or to be seen separately

- whatever choice they make will not be to the detriment of their case
- they should take legal advice if unsure of their position.

In cases in which violence between the parties has been alleged, a joint interview must not be convened if it can reasonably be foreseen that the safety or well-being of either party might be jeopardised.

Children at risk

During the course of your enquiries, if it becomes apparent that a child may be at risk of significant harm, the concern must be followed up and reported immediately in accordance with local child protection procedures. The court must be advised of the situation and you should suspend the enquiry pending further directions from the court.

Practice Direction 24 February 1984 [1984] FLR 356 states that welfare reports must be endorsed with the words:

This report has been prepared for the court and should be treated as confidential. It must not be shown nor its contents revealed to any person other than a party or a legal adviser to such a party. Such legal adviser may make use of the report in connection with an application for legal aid.

In the absence of a direction, your report should be submitted to the court 14 days before the hearing. You need not attend the hearing unless required to do so by the court.

Contents of the s. 7 report

Points to be addressed in a section 7 report include:

- the enquiries undertaken, including who was seen and where (missing appointments may be listed)
- the nature of the application which gave rise to the court-ordered enquiry
- the details of issues in dispute
- whether there is any measure of agreement between the parties

- whether there is any prospect of agreement being reached without the continued involvement of the court
- the present arrangements for the child
- the matters set out in the welfare checklist (see chapter eleven)
- the 'no-order' principle.

Options available to the court

The report should include a reasoned assessment of the options open to the court including:

- the parties' proposals
- their likely consequences
- the wishes and feelings of the children
- referral for mediation.

A recommendation is not required but should be included if you have formed a view about the appropriate course of action.

Family assistance order

In 'exceptional circumstances' (i.e. not routinely), a court may make a family assistance order under section 16, for six months or a shorter period. This requires a probation officer or social worker to advise, assist and (where appropriate) befriend any named person who may include:

- any parent (including the unmarried father) or guardian
- any person with whom the child is living or in whose favour a contact order is in force with respect to the child
- the child.

Before including a family assistance order in the options to be considered by the court, you must:

- identify clear plans for the work to be undertaken
- state how it will be achieved
- discuss the plan with the parties and obtain their consent
- take into account the child's wishes, although the child's consent is not required.

Inform the parties of your conclusions

Keep the parties aware of your emerging conclusions so that the final report does not hold any surprises. Inform them that it is for the court to provide them or their representatives with a copy of your report. They should be informed when the report is submitted to the court. Unrepresented parties should be told of their right to obtain a copy of the report from the court.

Power of the court to order an investigation

Section 37

(1) In family proceedings in which a question arises concerning the child's welfare, where it appears to the court that it may be appropriate for a care or supervision order to be made, the court may direct the appropriate authority to undertake an investigation of the child's circumstances.
(2) The local authority shall consider whether they should -
    (a) apply for a care or supervision order with respect to the child
    (b) provide services or assistance for the child or his family; or
    (c) take any other action with respect to the child.
(4) The information shall be given to the court before the end of *eight weeks* from the date of the direction, unless the court otherwise directs.

Purpose of s. 37 enquiry

No party may apply for a section 37 direction but parties in any family proceeding may suggest it to the court. A section 37 report should be ordered only where it appears to the court that a care or supervision order may be necessary. In an exceptional case, the court may make an interim care order[5].

The local authority's duty to investigate is set out in section 47. Under section 37, the authority must consider whether to apply for an order or exercise any of its other powers under the Act. These include making an offer of accommodation and applying for an emergency protection order.

Appointment of a guardian

A guardian ad litem may be involved if an interim order has been made or if the court is considering making such an order (section 41(6)(b)).

Planning the enquiry	In conducting a section 37 enquiry, you should:

In conducting a section 37 enquiry, you should:

- see the child unless there is enough information on which to base a decision (section 47(4))
- consider whether to consult housing, health and any other local authority (who are obliged to assist unless unreasonable for them to do so in all the circumstances of the case (section 47(5), (9)-(11)).[6]

If access is refused

If refused access to the child or denied information about his whereabouts, the authority should apply for an emergency protection order, child assessment order, care or supervision order unless satisfied that the child's welfare can be satisfactorily safeguarded without such an order (section 47(6)).

If no application is appropriate

If the conclusion of your investigation is not to apply for a care or supervision order with respect to the child, a consultation with the legal adviser may not be necessary. Discuss this with your manager. The report to the court need not be very detailed. It should address:

- the work undertaken for the investigation
- the reasons for the decision not to apply for an order
- the details of any service or assistance provided, or which it is intended to provide, for the child and his family; and
- any other action taken, or which it is proposed to take, with respect to the child
- whether it would be appropriate to review the case at a later date and, if so, the date on which the review is to begin (section 37 (6)).

1   Home Office (1994) National Standards for Probation Service Family Court Welfare Work.
2   Department of Health (1988) Protecting Children: A Guide for Social Workers undertaking a Comprehensive Assessment. HMSO.
3   16 July 1981 [1981] 2 All ER 1056.
4   Children Act Advisory Committee Annual Report 1993/94 pp. 59-63.
5   Re CE (Section 37 Direction) [1995] 1 FLR 26.
6   The Education Act 1993 repealed the application of this provision to education departments.

—8—

Content and layout

> Statements can be unnecessarily lengthy and sometimes it is hard to pick out the most important points. This chapter tries to help you make your statement succinct, relevant and easy to read.

Weigh what is relevant

Incorporate in your statement only what is directly relevant to the case. Does the information in question relate to:

- one of the guiding principles of the Children Act (see Figure 1 on page 5)
- the requirements of the Children Act section at issue
- giving a fair and balanced view
- a well-reasoned conclusion?

If the answer is 'no' to all of these questions, then the information probably need not be included.

> **Do not obscure the important points of your statement with unnecessary detail.**

The social worker's expertise

The law permits opinion evidence to be given by experts. At court, practitioners may give an opinion on matters within their observations and experience.

> **When you express an opinion, particularly in cases of suspected sexual abuse, do so within the limitations of your own expertise. If you exceed this you may be criticised by the court. Be clear about the factual basis for any opinion you express.**

Distinguish fact and opinion

In considering which facts are relevant and any opinion which you wish to add to your evidence, you should distinguish:

- matters to be described factually as a result of your direct observations

- your opinion or interpretation of behaviour or events which you have observed
- matters recorded on the file or told to you by others which are relevant to the case but which you cannot personally verify
- your opinion of the reasons for the order being sought and the care plan based on your overall professional experience.

Example comparing two descriptions of the same event:

'I made a home visit as a result of an anonymous phone call saying there was a child crying. When I got there, Mrs Callaghan let me in. Laurie was very distressed and clinging. It seemed to me that Mrs Callaghan had only recently returned and that Laurie had been left on her own. Mrs Callaghan denied this and said they had been out shopping together.'

The following description provides more graphic factual details as well as the basis for the social worker's opinion:

'Mrs Callaghan let me in. She had her coat on and there were two bags of shopping just inside the front door. Laurie was upstairs but I could hear her crying. Mrs Callaghan brought her down. Laurie was wearing a nightie which was wet with urine. She had no shoes on. Her face was puffy and blotchy and she was sobbing, gulping and hiccoughing. Laurie clung to Mrs Callaghan and would not let herself be put down or accept a bottle. I explained about the phone call. Mrs Callaghan said she had taken Laurie shopping and they had only just returned. I concluded, from Laurie's clothing and her emotional state, that the anonymous call was correct and that she had been left on her own for some time.'

Hearsay

Hearsay evidence relates to something not personally seen or heard by the witness. In order to remove the stress for children of giving evidence, court rules allow for hearsay evidence about what the child has said to be given by professional or lay adults[1].

When hearsay evidence is being reported, it should be clearly identified as such together with the circumstances

46

in which you received it. The court should be told the circumstances in which the hearsay originally came to light in order that it can make a fair judgement of the weight to be accorded to it.

In deciding the weight to attach to hearsay evidence, the court will consider:

- all the circumstances surrounding the making of the statement
- all the circumstances from which any inference can reasonably be drawn about the accuracy of the statement
- whether the statement was made at the same time that the incident occurred or was revealed
- whether the maker of the statement had any incentive to hide or misrepresent the facts
- whether the statement is corroborated by other evidence.

Example of an account of hearsay reported by Mrs Collis, foster carer for Jeanette Ward aged five, included in the social worker's statement:

'On 21.8.95, while Mrs Collis was bathing Jeanette and talking about dolls, Jeanette suddenly poked her arm with her finger and said, "my mummy does this". When asked what she meant, Jeanette replied, "prick with a needle".'

The social worker goes on to provide information to assist the court in deciding what weight to attach to the hearsay:

'Mrs Collis reports that Jeanette's remarks were spontaneous. Mrs Collis has never met Ms Ward and I know no reason why Mrs Collis would misrepresent this incident. Ms Ward acknowledges smoking cannabis but strongly denies using needles.'

Particular care is needed to avoid presenting the conclusions of others without supporting facts.

Examples of poor practice:

'Mrs Moston has a very explosive temper. In the view of some professionals who have previously worked with her, when she is under pressure she is likely to act irrationally.'

'The police officers were shocked and dismayed at the state of the home, particularly the provisions made for the children.'

'The foster placement broke down due to what the foster carer described as wild behaviour.'

'Mrs Thomas' family have in the past expressed concern about the children's behaviour, lack of parental supervision and poor school attendance.'

Duty to disclose information favourable to parents

The local authority's evidence must demonstrate that the course of action it proposes is in the child's best interests. This must not be achieved by including in its statements only those facts and opinions which support the local authority's position. The courts have clearly established that where the welfare of children is the paramount consideration, there is a duty on all parties to make full and frank disclosure of all matters relevant to welfare whether these are favourable or adverse to their own particular case. This includes the disclosure of information by local authorities to parents which may assist in rebutting allegations against them[2].

> **In *re B* [1994] 1 FCR 471 the mother's counsel criticised the evidence of the social worker as being selective in the material taken from the records to make up her statement. Hollings J said 'I cannot emphasise too much that applicants such as a local authority responsible for children in their care... should not act in a one hundred per cent adversarial way... they must present [the case] in a balanced way and not fail to refer, it seems deliberately, to factors which point in a direction opposite to that which is desired by the local authority.'**

Example acknowledging information favourable to a parent:

Ms Latimer's previous child was made the subject of a care order due to non-accidental injuries and was subsequently adopted; the present child Louise, aged two, is the subject of investigation for non-accidental injury.

While setting out reasons for concern about the recent deterioration in Ms Latimer's care of Louise, the statement nevertheless acknowledges that:

'An assessment of Ms Latimer's parenting skills after Louise's birth was conducted by the health visitor and social worker. They found a satisfactory standard of parenting and a warm and appropriate relationship between mother and daughter. This led to Louise's name being removed from the child protection register'.

Requests for disclosure to a criminal case

All requests to disclose information from social work records to a criminal case must be referred to the local authority legal adviser. This applies regardless of whether the request comes from the prosecution or the defence.

Referring to the parties

Refer to all adults as Mr, Mrs or Ms, not by their first names. It may also be helpful to specify the relationship in the text, for example "Mrs White (the children's maternal grandmother)".

The use of language

Your statement will be read by the parties, not just by the court and the lawyers. Jargon ('rehabilitation', for example) provides a form of short-hand for those with a common knowledge base, but its use is inappropriate in documents read by family members and children.

Unless central to decision-making about the child, avoid inflammatory comments, particularly in the context of what one party said about the other.

Use appropriate tenses and complete sentences throughout the statement.

Line spacing

Use a line spacing of at least 1½. Your document will be slightly longer but a great deal easier to read and absorb. Leave a blank line between paragraphs.

Statement pages should be single-sided.

Paragraph numbering

Numbered paragraphs make it easy to refer to specific parts of the document. Do not try to cover too much per paragraph. In general, deal with just one main point or idea and keep sentences fairly short. Where appropriate, begin a paragraph with a date. Avoid imprecise references to time such as 'during the summer' or 'at the weekend'.

Sub-headings

Sub-headings on a separate line are useful signposts for the reader to the content of the paragraphs that follow. If a statement is particularly long (over 12 pages) it may be helpful to provide an index to the subheadings and related paragraph numbers. The choice of subheadings must be governed by the content of your statement.

Exhibits

Consider whether there are any documents on file which should be attached to your statement, for example:

- a contract or agreement with the family
- an assessment report
- a letter from the child or parent.

Discuss with your legal adviser how these attachments should be marked as exhibits, numbered and cross-referenced.

Example:

Assessment by Pinetrees Family Centre: 'This is Exhibit 1 referred to in the second statement of social worker Diane Nixon dated 6.6.95'.

Controlling the number of updates

Since the implementation of the Children Act, most courts have experienced a significant increase in the amount of paperwork filed. It is not necessary to file a statement for every hearing. Before the final hearing it will be necessary to file a care plan and an updated statement may be appropriate if there have been significant changes.

> **Repetition of earlier material filed by the authority or by other witnesses or parties must be avoided. Cross-refer where appropriate.**

You will always be given the opportunity to update information at the beginning of your oral evidence. Discuss with your legal adviser whether this is appropriate in the circumstances.

Suggested statement contents

The local authority provides information to the court and the parties in stages, in its application and in subsequent statements. Information is often presented in a chronological narrative but it can be more accessible to the reader if organised by key issues.

The following list, cross-referenced to the relevant Children Act section and Handbook chapter, is not intended to be prescriptive:

Starting the document
Kevin (9)

---

1 Children (Admissibility of Hearsay Evidence) Order 1993 Statutory Instrument 1993/621.

2 For example, Thorpe J. in Essex County Council v R [1993] 2 FLR 826; Wall J. in Re D.H. (A Minor) (Child Abuse) [1994] 1 FLR 679; Watkins L.J. in R v Hampshire County Council ex parte K [1990] 1 FLR 330.

Figure 5: Selecting what should go into your statement

Subject	Children Act section	Handbook chapter
facesheet		9
the author's experience in social work and with this family		9
list of parties, family members and others mentioned in the statement		9
chronological history of key events (factual)		12
key information about court timetable		3
background to the proceedings		2, 10, 11
public law applications	25, 31, 39, 43 and 44	6
private law court ordered enquiries	7 and 37	7
information about the child	1(3)(b) and (d)	11
the wishes and feelings of the child	1(3)(a)	11
arrangements for contact	17, 23(6) and (7) and 34	13
working with parents and providing services	17	10
the parents' wishes and feelings	22(4) and (5)	10
assessment of risk factors	1(3)(e)	10
the capacity of the parents/ carers to meet the child's present needs	1(3)(f)	10
the care plan		14
the conclusion, including the options available to the court and the 'no order' principle	1(3)(g) and (5)	15

—9—

Starting the document

> **Effective presentation makes the content of your statement more accessible. This chapter provides examples of how to lay out:**
>
> - **the face sheet**
> - **the author's experience and involvement in the case**
> - **the list of parties, family members and others.**

The face sheet

On the first page, the statement should provide the following information:

- the name of the court dealing with the case
- case number (on transfer, the courts may give an additional number)
- child's name and date of birth
- type of Children Act application and relevant section
- the local authority applicant (some authorities also list the respondent parties by name)
- the name of the author, professional address and telephone number
- the date and number of the statement by this author (it may be one of a series).

Family Proceedings Rules 1991 declaration

The facesheet must incorporate a signed declaration that 'I, ... , social worker of .... , declare that this statement is true and that I make it knowing it may be placed before the court in these proceedings'.

Many authorities also include a notice of the confidential status of the statement.

Example:

THIS STATEMENT IS CONFIDENTIAL AND MUST NOT BE DISCLOSED WITHOUT THE CONSENT OF THE COURT

Author:
Statement No:
Dated:
On behalf of the applicant
Case No:

In the _____ Family Proceedings Court
In the matter of _____ d.o.b. _____
Children Act s. 31 application for a care or supervision order

between _____ County Council, applicant
and _____ First respondent
and _____ Second respondent
and _____ (child's name & d.o.b.) Third respondent

_____

Statement of Robert Whitaker, social worker

_____

I Robert Whitaker, social worker of _____ CC, declare that this statement is true and that I make it knowing it may be placed before the court in these proceedings.

Signed _____   Date _____

Author's experience

The statement should begin with a summary of your qualifications and relevant experience, for example:

BA 1985   CQSW 1992
1988-90   Junior school teacher
1992-94   Social worker _____   CC community team
1994-date   Social worker _____   CC child protection team

You should also describe the basis for your knowledge, for example:

'I make this statement based on my direct experience as the child's social worker since January 1994, and also on previous social work records. In describing recent events, I have drawn on information provided by WPC K. O'Neill and GP Dr M. Patel.'

Explain who's who

It is helpful to the court to open your statement with a list of parties to the proceedings, family members and other persons to whom you intend to refer. Where there is more than one family grouping, a family tree is particularly useful.

Ethnic minority names

Ask how the individual's name should be listed and which is the *personal* name, which (if any) is the *family* name and which is used as a *surname.* Do not assume that everyone will have a surname in the usual British sense or a family name, or that the family name will necessarily come last[1].

Photographs

Consider showing the court photographs of the child.

Example: Family tree

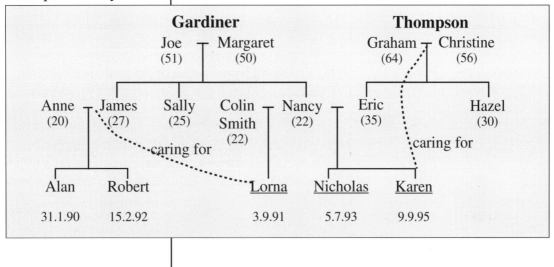

---

1 Judicial Studies Board Ethnic Minorities Advisory Committee (1994) Names and Naming Systems. A summary of this paper has been serialised as follows in The Magistrate:
   Names and Naming Systems, July/August 1994 p. 111
   Hindu Names, September 1994 p. 139
   Sikh Names, October 1994 pp. 158 and 168
   Muslim Names, November 1994 pp. 186 and 187
   Chinese Names, December 1994/January 1995 p. 209.

–10–

The parents

Your statement should describe how the local authority has discharged its responsibility to:

- **work with parents**
- **provide services**
- **consider the wishes and feelings of parents and others**
- **assess risk.**

> SECTION 17
>
> **The local authority has a duty to safeguard and promote the welfare of children in need in its area. As far as possible, this is best achieved by providing services appropriate to those children's needs to keep the family together.**

Providing services and working with parents

Given the high proportion of 'looked after' children who eventually return home from the care system[1], care proceedings should not divert a local authority from continuing its efforts to work in partnership with parents[2]. The Children Act Advisory Committee emphasises that both the local authority and the parents have 'a role to play, often simultaneously, in the case management of a child at risk'[3].

Your evidence should describe:

- details of the services, if any, offered or provided to this family
- the period over which services were offered or provided
- the response of the parents and the level of take-up of the services offered
- reasons given by the parents for refusing services
- agreements made with the parents

56

- why the provision of services on a voluntary basis is not considered adequate to safeguard the child's welfare
- how the local authority plans to work with the parents if an order is made.

SECTION *22(4) and (5)*

Before making any decision regarding a child whom they are looking after, or proposing to look after, a local authority shall, so far as is reasonably practicable, ascertain and give due consideration to the wishes and feelings of:

- **the parents**
- **anyone else with parental responsibility**
- **other relevant people.**

The way in which this consultation process was carried out and the responses of the child, family and others to the local authority action should be described in the local authority's evidence.

Assessing risk

The welfare checklist (section 1(3)) directs the court to pay particular regard to the potential risk to the child and the capacity of parents and relevant others to meet the child's needs. In assessing the child's situation and the likelihood of future harm, factors to be considered include[4]:

- evidence of previous injuries or abuse
- the risk of physical, sexual or emotional abuse or neglect
- serious personality problems or pathological patterns of behaviour
- evidence of the parents' capacity to change
- the degree of responsibility accepted by the parents for the child's situation
- the capacity of a non-abusing parent to protect the child
- whether there is someone within the family willing and able to protect the child.

You should weigh up to what extent the parents:

57

- recognise the need for help and will cooperate with those providing it
- show affection to the child and put the child's needs first
- are capable of sticking to agreed arrangements.

Explaining to the child
Lucy (7)

1   Bullock R., Little M. and Millham S. (1993) Going Home. Dartmouth Press, Aldershot.

2   Department of Health (1991) The Children Act 1989 Guidance and Regulations Volume 3, Family Placements para. 2.19. HMSO.

3   Annual Report 1992/93 p. 34.

4   Timms J. (1995) Children's Representation - A Practitioner's Guide. Sweet and Maxwell. Pp. 166-167.

–11–

The child

> This chapter discusses the welfare principle and the welfare checklist giving particular attention to the child's :
>
> - background
> - wishes and feelings.
>
> The use of centile charts is explained.

The welfare principle - the child's welfare is paramount

SECTION 1(1)

Before taking any decision, the court must put the child's welfare first.

The welfare checklist

SECTION 1(3)

The court is directed to pay particular regard to the following factors:

- the wishes and feelings of the child concerned (considered in the light of his age and understanding)
- his physical, emotional and educational needs
- the likely effect on him of any change in his circumstances
- his age, sex, background and any characteristics of his which the court considers relevant
- any harm which he has suffered or is at risk of suffering
- how capable each of his parents, and any other person in relation to whom the court considers the question to be relevant, is of meeting his needs
- the range of powers available to the court under the Children Act in the proceedings in question.

Scope of the welfare checklist

Courts must consider the checklist in all applications relating to local authority care and supervision of children and in contested section 8 order applications (sections 1(4), 8(4)). In other applications, you may wish to address the welfare checklist in your statement as an aid to the court's decision making. The checklist can be a useful test of relevance in deciding what should be included in your written evidence but it is not exhaustive.

Harm is discussed in chapter six. Risk and parental capacity are dealt with in chapter ten.

Give due consideration to the child's background

Section 22(5)(c)

Before making any decision regarding a child whom they are looking after, or proposing to look after, a local authority shall, so far as is reasonably practicable, ascertain and give due consideration to the child's:

- **racial**
- **cultural**
- **religious**
- **linguistic**

background.

Effective action to prevent discrimination requires significantly more than a willingness to accept all people as equal or to invest an equal amount of time and effort in different cases. To ensure that families from a different background are not disadvantaged, the origin, nature and extent of differences in circumstances and need must be properly understood and addressed.

Example alerting the court to concerns about language and the family's ability to communicate:

'During the period of the interim care orders a communication difficulty has arisen between Shamim (aged three) and his mother Mrs Khan. Shamim has forgotten his native language and his English is sometimes better than his mother's. Mrs Khan tries to speak English to Shamim and Urdu to Ali (aged eighteen months).'

Examples from family members interviewed by the Family Rights Group[1]:

'We are two totally different cultures ... They expect children to be brought up in a white middle class way. We have different ways of disciplining our children, teaching them, playing with them ... We give them more responsibilities in life. They are using it in the wrong way because of the differences and looking at my culture negatively and not taking into account that we are different and that my culture may be the reason for doing things in a particular way.'

'Social services and the court gave very little attention to our race and culture in arranging the children's care and reaching a decision. The court should have had some evidence of cultural background ... The court should make room for people who come from different cultural backgrounds.'

Being well informed is essential in order to make a proper assessment of what is in the best interests of children. You should:

- ask families about life-styles, child rearing and cultural patterns and expectations of service[2]
- acknowledge the importance of the family's own traditions[3]
- explain any relevant social or cultural factors which may not otherwise be understood by the court
- identify sources of advice and help so that the necessary experience, expertise and resources are available where needed.

Give due consideration to wishes and feelings

SECTION 22(4) and (5)

Before making any decision regarding a child whom they are looking after, or proposing to look after, a local authority shall, so far as is reasonably practicable, ascertain and give due consideration to the wishes and feelings of the child (having regard to age and understanding).

61

The way in which this task was approached and the response of the child to the local authority action should be described in your evidence.

> **UN Convention on the Rights of the Child Article 12**
>
> **1. States Parties shall assure to the child who is capable of forming his or her own views the right to express those views freely in all matters affecting the child, the views of the child being given due weight in accordance with the age and maturity of the child.**
>
> **2. For this purpose, the child shall in particular be provided the opportunity to be heard in any judicial and administrative proceedings affecting the child, either directly or through a representative or an appropriate body, in a manner consistent with the procedural rules of national law.**

Referring to percentile charts

Where a child may be failing to thrive, the health visitor should be asked to put together a centile chart for the child and to document any investigations into whether there are organic reasons for concern. Is the child passing the developmental milestones of babyhood and childhood?

Preprinted percentile (or centile) charts provide information about the average height, weight and head circumference for a child of a given age. The data are displayed on five lines, the middle of which is the average, or 50th centile. This means that 50 per cent of children have measurements above and 50 per cent below these figures. The other lines show the 97th, 90th, 10th and third centiles.

The starting point for screening purposes is to consider children at the third and 97th centile as outside the norm. Although further investigation of children in these cut-off areas is appropriate, not all will turn out to be abnormal.

Percentile charts are used to plot the weight of an individual child over time. The pattern of growth over time is important, particularly where this departs from the norm. Once a child has reached the age of four months and has established a pattern of growth, he or she is likely to remain on the centile. If the chart shows that the child's weight, height or a baby's head circumference is falling away from the centile formerly followed, this gives rise to concerns of physical and/or emotional deprivation unless the loss is caused by organic illness. It is important to continue to chart the weight changes of children in care as 'failure to thrive' may be followed by 'catch up' growth suggestive of a change in the child's well-being[4].

> **The interpretation of percentile charts is the responsibility of medical professionals.**

Making my voice heard
Martin (13)

1 Lindley B. (1994) On the Receiving End: families' experiences of the court process in care and supervision proceedings under the Children Act 1989. Family Rights Group, pp. 56-57.

2 Department of Health (1991) The Children Act 1989 Guidance and Regulations Volume 3 Family Placements paras. 2.57, 2.71. HMSO.

3 Department of Health (1995) Challenge of Partnership in Child Protection: Practice Guide para. 2.60. HMSO.

4 A Child in Trust (1985) Report of the Panel of Inquiry into the circumstances surrounding the death of Jasmine Beckford. London Borough of Brent pp. 70-72.

The chronology

> The chronology provides the court with a diary of key events and is often the first-read document at the final hearing. The preparation of the chronology may be undertaken either by the social worker or legal adviser.
>
> The chronology is most useful if prepared and submitted early in the proceedings. It is then available:
>
> - as an introduction to the case for the bench at interim hearings
> - as a reference when drafting local authority statements
> - to assist the guardian ad litem's enquiries.
>
> If it is necessary to update the chronology, an addendum can be submitted prior to the final hearing.

The chronology provides a skeleton of the events which led up to the proceedings. It brings together factual information from the child protection register as well as from social work, medical and educational sources. It should:

- be succinct
- clearly identify key facts which can be agreed by all parties
- contain no opinion or judgement.

Events to be included in the chronology will depend on the circumstances of the case but may include:

- family history including marriages, births, deaths and changes in the make-up of the household
- the child's changes of address and school
- dates of case conferences and child protection registration
- key planning meetings
- relevant medical examinations

- incidents giving rise to concern
- child protection investigations
- history of children being accommodated voluntarily
- history of court applications, hearings and orders.

Example of a chronology used to set out the stages of an investigation:

19 December 1994	*While staying overnight with her aunt Mrs. K., Yasmin made allegations of sexual assault against her stepfather Mr Y. Mrs K. called the police.*
20 December 1994	*Yasmin was jointly interviewed by Detective Sergeant R. Williams and social worker Ms L. Suhani. During this interview, which was videotaped, Yasmin repeated the allegations.*
20 December 1994	*Yasmin was jointly examined by paediatrician Dr Sowerby and police surgeon Dr Griffiths at St Martin's Hospital.*
21 December 1994	*Mr Y. was interviewed by Detective Sergeant Williams through an interpreter. Mr Y denied the allegations. He was released on police bail and went to live with his brother.*
5 January 1995	*Mr Y was charged with four counts of indecent assault on his stepdaughter Yasmin.*

Example of a chronology used in tracing the child's movements in and out of accommodation:

29 October 1994	*Ms Vera Wilson left Rosie (then aged 4 months) in the care of her neighbours the Rowland family. After two days, Mrs Rowland called the emergency duty team. Rosie was accommodated voluntarily with foster parents Mr and Mrs Ellis.*

26 November 1994	*Mrs Ellis had to go into hospital so Rosie was moved to foster parent Mrs Drummond.*
10 January 1995	*Ms Wilson removed Rosie from Mrs Drummond's care. They went to live in a hostel for the homeless.*
15 April 1995	*At the request of her maternal grandmother Mrs Anne Wilson, who had taken care of Rosie overnight, Rosie was accommodated with foster parents Mr and Mrs Harris for five days.*
16-18 May 1995	*Rosie was accommodated for two days at her mother's request with foster mother Mrs Newlands; Ms Wilson did not collect her.*
18 May 1995	***Emergency Protection Order application; order made by the family proceedings court.***

– 13 –

The local authority plan for contact

> This chapter describes key issues concerning contact to be addressed in the local authority's care plan, other aspects of which are discussed in the next chapter. The Children Act emphasises the responsibility of the local authority:
>
> - to promote the upbringing by their families of children who are in need (section 17)
> - to enable children to live with their parents, relatives or friends (section 23(6))
> - to place children near their home and together with their brothers and sisters (section 23(7))
> - to allow reasonable contact between a child in the care of the authority and
>   persons for whom there is a statutory presumption of contact
>   others with whom contact will benefit the child (section 34).
>
> Local authority proposals are likely to be scrutinised closely at both interim and final hearings in most Children Act cases, because the Act gives the court the power to specify the nature of contact including frequency, duration and venue.

Contact integral to the care plan

The interests of the majority of children are best served by efforts to sustain or create links with their natural family. There is a presumption that it will be in the child's interests to have contact with his or her parents. Contact should be seen as an integral part of the overall care plan for each child rather than as an issue to be decided separately.

Clarity of purpose essential

Your plan must be clear about the purpose of contact for the child in question. This has to be assessed solely in terms of the child's interests. Contact which is working towards rehabilitation is likely to differ from contact which serves to maintain some links but is working towards permanency elsewhere.

> **Contacts, however occasional, may continue to have a value for the child even where there is no question of returning to the family.**

Contact can keep alive for a child a sense of his origins and may keep open options for family relationships later in life[1]. 'We find balm and comfort applied to the wounds of separation when they should be kept open and salted'[2]. Where face to face contact is likely to be harmful to the child, other forms of contact should be explored.

Presumption of contact with wide network

> **Ensure that you have full information about the network of relatives and friends important to the child.**

For children looked after under a court order or in accommodation, the local authority must 'endeavour to promote contact' between children and their parents, guardians, anyone else with parental responsibility, relatives, friends and others connected with them, such as teachers, unless it is not reasonably practicable or consistent with the child's welfare[3].

Even where it is proposed to terminate contact between the child and parents, there remains a presumption that contact will be maintained with grandparents, brothers and sisters.

There is a presumption of contact not just with full brothers and sisters but also with half and step siblings, although the level and intensity of the need for contact should be considered for each relationship. The question of whose welfare is paramount in this area can be complex, especially if private, public and adoption law issues intermingle. It is advisable to seek legal advice.

The presumption of contact between parent and child applies not only to care proceedings but also when the

68

child is the subject of an emergency protection or child assessment order.

If the local authority is seeking to overturn the presumption of contact, it must show why contact is not in the best interests of the child or why it will be disruptive[4].

SECTION 34

(1) Requires the authority to allow the child reasonable contact with his parents or guardian, or a person who, immediately prior to the making of the care order, had care of the child under a residence order or an order of the High Court.

(2) On an application made by the authority or the child, the court may make such an order as it considers appropriate with respect to the contact which is to be allowed between the child and any named person.

(4) On an application made by the authority or the child, the court may make an order authorising the authority to refuse to allow contact between the child and any named person who is mentioned in section 34(1) and named in the order.

'Reasonable' contact is objective test of child's welfare

For children looked after under a court order, the local authority must allow reasonable contact with parents, guardians and anyone with a residence order. 'Reasonable' means 'objectively reasonable' which is not the same as contact at the local authority's discretion[5]. The court can order contact with a child in care even if it conflicts with the local authority's long-term plans, but only if contact is necessary for the child's welfare. The court will expect the parent to prove this[6].

Consultation is necessary

In order to encourage consultation and agreements about contact which all parties can accept as 'reasonable', before making a care order the court must invite the parties to comment on the local authority's proposals for contact (section 34(11)). Your plan should identify key persons in the child's life and describe what steps have been taken to consult, not merely to inform, them about proposed contact arrangements[7].

Contact plan to inform placement decision

Where possible, arrangements for contact should be made before the child is placed. The need for contact should inform the decision about what placement would be best for the child.

Details of the contact plan

Visits should enable parents and others to engage in normal everyday activities with their children. The plan must consider the short- and long-term goals of contact. Issues to be addressed include[8]:

- the child's wishes
- contact in the short- and long-term
- any agreement reached by the parties about contact or efforts to reach agreement
- frequency and length of sessions
- whether supervision is necessary and, if so, by whom
- transportation (arrangements for the child and those with whom contact is proposed)
- escort for the child while being transported
- details of the advice and support to be provided to parents to maximise the benefits of the contact to the child
- provisions for financial help to support visits[9]
- whether overnight stays are appropriate and if so, who else is likely to be in the house overnight.

Setting

State where contact should take place and give reasons if the home of the person seeking contact is not appropriate. The court can only order contact at a specific venue if it is the property of the local authority or a willing agent.

The purpose of supervision

If the local authority proposes that visits should be supervised, the plan should be clear about why this is necessary and give some indication of for how long supervision is contemplated. If supervision is part of an assessment of the parent - child relationship or of the ability to parent, then the plan should make clear the purpose of the assessment and provide the qualifications of the worker(s) involved.

If supervision is, alternatively, to ensure that some behaviour does not occur, the concerns need to be made clear in the contact plan. Appropriate persons to perform this supervisory task may include relatives and family friends.

Review of contact provisions

Contact plans should specify:

- when they will be reviewed and by whom[10]
- how the parents and child will participate
- that arrangements, including supervision of sessions, will be reviewed to ensure that they are not unnecessarily restrictive[11].

The monitoring of the contact plan should take into account the possibility that a particular placement may need to be changed because it is interfering with the maintenance of good contact.

Taking account of circumstantial barriers to contact

For school-age children, contact is likely to be offered after school. For parents and other family members, evening or weekend contact may be more desirable. The plan should be as flexible as possible and take account of problems arising from distance, lack of public transport, cost of travel and commitment to other children at home.

> **The plan should be creative in addressing ways to maintain contact between children and families. Practical support should be provided before a judgement is made as to whether parents are motivated to maintain links. Families should be told if their motivation is being tested.**

Contact may take many forms

If your plan does not propose face-to-face meetings, alternative arrangements should be considered such as letters, cards, phone calls, reasonable presents and exchange of photographs. Frequency and routeing (i.e. direct or through a named intermediary) should be considered. Parents are likely to require advice about what is appropriate in these circumstances.

Restricting contact

Section 34(6) empowers an authority to refuse to allow contact as a matter of urgency (i.e. as a result of a recent problem, not to solve long-standing difficulties) for not more than seven days. In order to extend this period it is necessary to apply for an order under section 34(4).

If you consider that the child has valid reasons for not wanting contact with someone, you should seek legal advice about whether it should be the local authority or the child who makes the application to stop contact (section 34(4)).

Where contact is to be terminated, sensitive arrangements need to be made for farewell visits.

Children's experience of contact visits

> **Children are likely to manifest distress or difficult behaviour before, during and after contact sessions. In describing such behaviour to the court, it is important to be objective and to take account of possible different reasons for such behaviour.**

The plan should address the need to support children, families and carers to cope with upset resulting from contact so that they can continue to visit or support the visits[12].

It is important to obtain the views of the child, parents, supervisor and foster carer about the contact sessions.

Openness in adoption

Consider carefully whether a 'clean break' is in the best interests of the child. Adoption with contact will not automatically impede the child's bonding with the new family. Children are capable of forming new relationships and attachments without necessarily having to shed existing ones[13].

Openness can take many different forms. What is appropriate will vary according to the needs of the child and the circumstances of the adoption[14]. Where openness is in the child's best interests, the local authority must seek suitable adoptive parents with the specific needs of the child in mind[15].

Contact may be more appropriate for older children who already have a strong relationship with a relative. However, some older children may want to make a completely clean break. On the other hand, some adoptive parents of younger children may feel that it is in the child's interests to grow up having occasional contact with his or her mother. The child's wishes about contact may change significantly as he or she grows up. The child may come to feel overwhelming commitment to the adoptive family and draw back from contact, or may decide after several years to seek contact with a relative for the first time[16].

Case law on adoption with contact is technical and restrictive[17]. A contact order in adoption will only be made in exceptional circumstances, where the natural parent consents to the adoption and the adopters consent to the condition. Legal advice should be sought before making a recommendation.

1   Department of Health (1991) The Children Act 1989 Guidance and Regulations Volume 3, Family Placements para. 6.9. HMSO.

2   Millham S., Bullock R., Hosie K., and Haak M., (1986) Lost in Care: the problems of maintaining links between children in care and their families. Gower. P. 232.

3   Children Act Schedule 2, para. 15(1).

4   Re M (Care: Contact: Grandmother's application for leave) [1995] 2 FLR 86.

5   Re P (Minors) (Contact with Children in Care) [1993] 2 FLR 156.

6   Re B (Minors) (Termination of Contact: Paramount Consideration) [1993] 1 FLR 543.

7   Department of Health (1995) Looking after Children Placement Plan Part Two: 5.

8   Department of Health (1995) Looking after Children Placement Plan Part One: 11-13; Placement Plan Part Two: 5.

9   Children Act Schedule 2 para. 16.

10 Department of Health (1995) Looking after Children Care Plan: 19-22.

11 Department of Health (1991) The Children Act Guidance and Regulations Volume 3, Family Placements para. 6.38. HMSO.

12 Ryan M. (1994) The Children Act 1989 Putting it into Practice. Chapter 7: Contact. Arena.

13 Wedge P. and Thoburn J. (1986) Finding Families for 'Hard-to-Place' Children - evidence from research. British Association for Adoption and Fostering.

14 Department of Health and Welsh Office (1992) Review of Adoption Law - Report to Ministers of an Interdepartmental Working Group - A Consultation Document para. 4.2.

15 Re E (A Minor) (Contact) (1993) Fam 671.

16 Department of Health and Welsh Office (1992) Review of Adoption Law - Report to Ministers of an Interdepartmental Working Group - A Consultation Document paras. 5.2 and 5.3.

17 For example, re T (A Minor) (Contact Order) (1995) FCR 537. Under section 1(5), the court should not make an order unless doing so is better than making no order. Although a contact order could have been beneficial to the mother, it was to the benefit of the adopted child that her new parents should not feel that they were acting under constraint in doing what they had already agreed to do.

–14–

The local authority plan for care of the child

> When considering a local authority application, the court expects to receive a plan containing:
>
> - clear objectives for the care of children
> - a strategy for their achievement.
>
> There is no prescribed format for a care plan submitted in court proceedings. However, the courts have advised local authorities to set out the care plan in light of the elements listed in paragraph 2.62, Volume 3 of the Department of Health *Guidance and Regulations*. These elements are addressed in expanded form in this chapter.
>
> Plans for contact are an integral part of the care plan (see previous chapter).

Look to the future

Nearly 60 per cent of children looked after by local authorities return to their families within six months and 87 per cent go home within five years. Unless there are clear indications that restoration to the family is not a viable option, care plans should be made with the possibility of eventual return in mind[1].

The need for a plan

An initial plan must be submitted in support of an application for a section 31 care or supervision order[2]. The local authority will also be expected to provide a plan later in the proceedings and when applying for other orders. It may be appropriate for the care plan to be endorsed by a social services manager.

The court has a duty to scrutinise critically the care plan to satisfy itself that it will promote the child's welfare. With the exception of contact, the court cannot compel the local authority to follow a particular plan, even where the guardian ad litem is not in agreement with the local authority view. The court's only sanction is to refuse to make a care order.

One plan per child

A separate plan is needed for each child involved.

'Looked after' children

For those children who are already being looked after by the local authority, relevant information is recorded in the Department of Health system *Looking After Children* which is being implemented in a phased programme across local authorities[3].

The following forms in the *Looking After Children* system highlight elements of the care plan recorded by the local authority which are required by the court:

The Care Plan
Placement Plan Part One: Placement agreement
Placement Plan Part Two: Day-to-day arrangements
The Review of Arrangements.

Tailoring supporting evidence to the needs of case

A properly constructed care plan is essential to enable the court to take into account all known facts when making its decision. The amount of evidence that should be presented in support of the plan will vary from case to case. Mr Justice Wall stated that it was for the good sense of the court and the advocates to:

> 'strike a proper balance between the need to satisfy the court as to the appropriateness of the care plan and over-zealous investigation into matters properly within the local authority's administrative discretion. It should be rare for the court's dissatisfaction with the plan to be such as to prevent the making of the final care order in a case where it was satisfied both as to the threshold criteria and that a care order was in the child's best interests.'[4]

Is the care plan viable?

> **The care plan should:**
>
> - **identify the child's best interests**
> - **address the least detrimental alternative for the child**
> - **be based on a realistic allocation of resources.**
>
> **It may be necessary to acknowledge that a particular level of service is not available for resource reasons. Avoid describing a resource-led decision as being in the child's best interests unless it is so.**

The overall plan	Tell the court whether the overall plan for this child includes:

- time limited assessment
- remaining with the family through provision of support services, including respite care
- return to the birth family within one month/ six months/ eventual return (indicate within how many months)
- living with relatives/ friends
- supported living in the community
- independent living
- special residential placement (e.g. hospital unit)
- long-term placement with foster carers (no return to the birth family is anticipated)
- other services to be provided by the authority or other agencies
- adoption
- other (specify).

If a placement has been found, provide:

- the address (if appropriate to disclose this information)
- information about supporting the placement
- its expected duration and how long the child will need to be looked after by the local authority
- the contingency plan if the preferred placement is not available or breaks down
- arrangements for ending a voluntary placement.

Long term-needs

What long-term needs does the child have which the placement must meet? The following issues must be considered:

- ongoing physical and mental health conditions, illnesses or disabilities
- education
- identity - the child's gender, disability, ethnic origin, language and communication, religion or culture.

Key tasks

What needs to be done before this plan can be achieved? Identify:

- who has overall responsibility
- the key tasks

- who is assigned to carry them out
- target dates.

What is the day-to-day role of the parent(s) in relation to the child?

If any of the child's needs cannot be met at present, identify:

- what plans will be made to meet them in future
- the priority needs and how should they be addressed.

The plan must consider arrangements for contact (see the previous chapter).

Notification

The care plan should be notified in writing to the parents, the child, other carers, representatives of other agencies involved with the child and others with a sufficient interest in the child. Parents and children should be given a personal explanation of what the plan entails and the reasoning behind it[5], particularly if the long term plan is adoption.

Reviewing the plan

The care plan must specify:

- the time and location of the first review
- whether the carers and parents have been given the dates and venues of all reviews and planning meetings
- the names of those with whom the plan has been discussed
- the explanation why any of those listed have not been consulted or why they disagree with any provisions of the plan
- details of the social worker and family placement worker, the frequency with which they will visit the placement and the details of the team leader/ duty officer
- details of person(s) with authority to give consent to emergency and routine medical treatment including dental care; whether there is signed parental consent to medical treatment; whether the carers have been given a copy of the statutory medical report
- the signed consent[6] (and any further comments) of the parents and child in relation to a request for accommodation.

The *Review of Arrangements* form in the Department of Health system *Looking After Children* contains relevant information.

Plan for fostering

Where the plan is for foster placement and prospective carers have been identified, it may be appropriate for evidence about their suitability to be supplied by a social worker who knows them sufficiently well. The foster carers themselves need not give evidence[7].

Plan for adoption

The Children Act Advisory Committee has taken the view that:

> 'Care plans should be as full as the facts of an individual case allow. For example, where a permanent substitute family is planned, it is helpful if a range of possible adopters are identified and there is no reason why the Adoption Panel should not have become involved so long as the child has not been directly involved e.g. in meetings or placement. The crucial distinction is between planning in advance of the court's decision (which is to be encouraged) and on the other hand pre-empting the decision of the court... Local authorities should have these matters in mind when preparing the care plan in order to avoid unnecessary delay.'[8]

However, where there is no readily identifiable pool of suitable adopters for the child in question, the process of searching for an appropriate family must be described. Where the plan recommends placement for adoption, Mr Justice Wall considered that general evidence about the ease or difficulty of identifying a placement for the child will normally suffice[9]. This suggests that prior consultation (at a minimum) with the principal officer of the adoption or family placement section is appropriate.

Time estimates

Local authorities are often invited to estimate the time it will take to place a child for adoption. Those involved in court proceedings are likely to be unfamiliar with the sequence of steps required. Although it is impossible to forecast the total length of time needed to place an individual child, the authority should be able to give approximate times for the following stages, based on local experience:

- the completion of Form E
- submission of the child's name to the adoption panel for a decision concerning the child's best interests
- looking within the county for families already approved
- contact with other agencies
- identification of suitable families
- matching and approval by the adoption panel
- introductions between the child and prospective adopters.

1   Bullock R., Little M. and Millham S. (1993) Going Home. Dartmouth Press, Aldershot.

2   Form C 13, question 3; Family Proceedings Courts (Children Act 1989) (Amendment) (No.4) Rules 1994.

3   See also Department of Health (1995) Looking After Children: Good Parenting, Good Outcomes - Management and Implementation Guide. HMSO.

4   Re J (A Minor) (Care Plan) [1994] 1 FLR 253.

5   Department of Health (1991) The Children Act 1989 Guidance and Regulations Volume 3, Family Placements para. 2.70. HMSO.

6   There is no legal requirement for the parent(s) or child to sign this form.

7   Re J (op. cit.).

8   Children Act Advisory Committee Annual Report 1993/1994, p. 32.

Coming to a conclusion

The conclusion constitutes your professional judgement and is the most important part of your submission to the court. If you are comfortable that your conclusion is based on accurate information set out in the body of the statement and that you have applied the appropriate principles, it will be easier to cope with cross-examination at court.

This chapter contains suggestions about:

- reaching a well-reasoned conclusion
- reviewing your statement.

Justifying your conclusion

Make the conclusion flow from the rest of the statement

The document should make it clear to the reader how you arrived at your conclusions. Have you demonstrated the factual basis for each part of your conclusion? In assessing the risk to the child, have you explained what would need to change for the child not to suffer significant harm within the home?

Set out the options available to the court and assess each in turn. Your position on each option should be substantiated by the evidence in the body of the statement. Drawing these together is likely to assist the court in its own analysis and in drafting reasons for its decisions.

The 'no order' principle - is any order necessary?

Section 1(5)

When reaching its decision, the court must be sure that an order will benefit the child. If the court cannot be certain of this, it must make no order at all.

The Children Act acknowledges that where possible, the best place for children to be brought up and cared for is within their own family. The Act aims to discourage court action where problems can be addressed by negotiation and to focus attention on those cases where a court order is necessary to secure the child's welfare.

When the local authority asks the court to make an order, its written evidence must demonstrate that the proposed care plan cannot be implemented without the benefit of court intervention.

The court has the power to make orders other than those applied for.

Even where there is parental agreement to the local authority plan, the statement should address:

- the extent of agreement
- whether the authority feels confident that agreement will be maintained
- whether the authority should share parental responsibility because of the risk to the child.

Take account of parties' views

The conclusions of other parties should be taken into account and the reasons for differences of opinion should be clearly recorded.

Based on your analysis, present a recommendation where appropriate to do so. It may not be appropriate to put forward a 'hard and fast' position at an early stage. Giving a provisional opinion in an early statement allows for a later change of position, where justified, and is likely to be seen as more balanced and reasonable.

Develop your recommendation as a result of consultation

Describe the consultation process which has led to your recommendation. Key decisions should be taken in consultation with managers and others in the multi-disciplinary network and after consultation with the child and the family.

Discuss with the guardian

At the time of submitting your final statement, you are unlikely to have received the report of the guardian ad litem. You should, however, have discussed the options available to the court with the guardian. Where you both reach different conclusions, be clear about your reasons for doing so. A difference of opinion with the guardian of itself does not require the local authority to change its position before the final hearing.

Facilitate conciliation

Not all significant harm is caused by malicious intent. Wherever possible, frame your proposals in a way which takes a compassionate view of the parents as work is likely to continue with them whether or not an order is made.

Consider whether your recommendation:

- is realistic and clearly explained

- is well-founded in the body of the statement

- takes account of the welfare checklist

- explains why the court should not apply the 'no order' principle.

Reviewing your statement

Look over the document

Always review what you have written. It is helpful if you can get a colleague to look at it as well. As you read, consider whether your statement:

- is well-focused

- takes account of the guiding principles of the Children Act as appropriate (see Figure 1 on page 5)

- reflects the requirements of the relevant section of the Act (chapters six or seven)

- is balanced and fair overall, giving credit where it is due to family members

- includes all relevant facts whether or not they support the local authority's conclusion

- verifies significant facts and justifies opinions

83

- avoids unnecessary repetition of material available in other court documents

- presents information with sensitivity, particularly in the context of what one party said about the other, unless central to decision-making about the child

- makes references to race, nationality, colour or country of origin which are relevant to the context

- avoids applying your own cultural or moral values to other cultures (assumptions may be implicit in your choice of words)

- takes account of changes that have occurred in the period leading up to the final hearing.

Louise (9)

–16– Giving evidence at court

> **Your written statement is likely to be regarded as your evidence in chief at court. This chapter suggests ways to:**
>
> - **present evidence authoritatively**
> - **help the court to incorporate your evidence into its decisions.**

Prepare for court

Before the court hearing, set aside enough time (see chapter three) for:

Refresh your memory about the details

- a discussion of the presentation of the case with your legal representative
- getting up to date with the other parties' views
- reading and organising the file (no loose papers)
- flagging any papers to which you may wish to refer while in the witness box
- reading your own statement
- reading all other statements and the guardian's report.

If you identify that any part of your statement is inaccurate or inconsistent, tell your legal adviser. Errors must be clarified to the court at the outset of your evidence.

Acknowledge areas of agreement

During court proceedings, the parents' legal representatives may make a point of stressing differences between their position and that of the local authority. Consider carefully alternative interpretations put forward in the statements of other parties and try to identify areas of agreement. Where you have come to a different conclusion from the other parties, be ready to explain the reasons for your disagreement. Acknowledging points about which there is no real dispute will assist you in giving a balanced presentation.

It is usually apparent from the other parties' statements what facts are in dispute or 'at issue', but if you are in any doubt, discuss this with your legal adviser. The questions

On the day

In the witness box

Joe (8)

you will be asked at court are most likely to concern the facts 'at issue'. Think ahead about all relevant facts which will clarify your position.

Present yourself professionally:

* bring your file
* dress appropriately for the formality of the proceedings
* punctuality is vital and if at all possible, arrive ahead of the scheduled start of court, as important decisions are often made in pre-court discussions.

The social worker witness is usually allowed to be present in court when not giving evidence.

Where the local authority is the applicant, its legal representative presents an outline of the case and calls its witnesses first. They will be asked to give their job title and professional address. When witnesses give evidence by replying to questions from their own legal representative, this is called evidence in chief. However, it is likely that your statement will be treated as your evidence in chief to save time.

The authority has the burden of proving its case on the balance of probabilities, i.e. that it is more likely than not. This is a lower standard of proof than in the criminal courts, where the prosecution must prove its case beyond reasonable doubt.

You will be asked to go into the witness box and take the oath or a non-religious affirmation. As an expert witness, your primary responsibility is to assist the court in making the best decision for the child. Any other loyalties, however proper, are secondary.

Call the magistrates 'sir' or 'madam'. A High Court judge is called 'My Lord' or 'My Lady'. All other judges are 'Your Honour'.

> **Three key techniques will make you seem at ease in the witness box, even if it is the first time you give evidence:**
>
> - **speak out clearly (practise using a confident, level tone of voice when you take the oath or affirm)**
> - **when you speak, turn to face the magistrates or judge, not the lawyer asking questions**
> - **pause periodically, allowing those taking notes to catch up (watch the pen!).**

Cross examination

In cross-examination, you are questioned by the legal representatives of all the other parties in turn. Social work evidence often concerns the interpretation of past behaviour and risk assessment. Make your oral evidence as factual as possible. The court can then assess the factual basis for your conclusions. Try to separate out the points you wish to make.

Listen very carefully to the questions. If you do not understand a question, ask for it to be explained. If the question asks for a response which is beyond your area of expertise or relates to an aspect of the case for which you have no responsibility or personal knowledge, state this clearly.

When responding to questions:

- take a balanced view - where possible, find something positive to say about the parents (such as their willingness to admit social workers conducting home visits) and acknowledge their positive feelings for the child, even if arguing that their parenting skills are not good enough
- if you are led to say something you did not really mean or which gives the wrong impression, set the record straight immediately
- do not feel obliged to change your answer, if it is accurate, simply because you are asked the same question in a different form
- hold your ground where appropriate, but do not be afraid to concede a valid point made to you in cross-examination

• do not argue - it is the lawyer's job to test your evidence.

Risk assessment

Giving a prognosis for the child's future is always difficult. Again, it is important to present your conclusions in a factual and balanced way, specifying the information on which your assessment is based.

Refer to your notes

If you cannot remember an answer which is nevertheless contained in your records, you may request the court's permission to refer to your own case notes in the file. You will be asked if you made the notes when the incidents were fresh in your mind. If you ask to refer to notes, the other parties' legal representatives are entitled to ask to look at them, though they may elect not to do so. Discuss whether you may wish to consult your notes with your legal adviser and manager before court.

After court

Check that family members understand what has happened at court. Some people not in the courtroom, including children and foster carers, will be anxiously waiting to hear the outcome of the proceedings. Ensure that they are notified as soon as possible, even if it means making a phone call after office hours.

References

Brayne H. and Martin G. (1994) Law for Social Workers. Chapter 8 - How to Behave in Court: Giving Evidence. Blackstone Press Ltd.

British Agencies for Adoption and Fostering (1992) Developing Your Court Skills. BAAF London.

Expert Testimony: Developing Witness Skills (training package with videos and printed booklets) British Psychological Society, 48 Princess Road East, Leicester.

Annex

Checklist for foster carers

> This checklist aims to assist foster carers in planning the content of their statements prior to discussion with the local authority legal adviser.

Experience as a foster carer

Tell the court about:

- the members of your household and ages of your children
- the number of years' experience you have as a foster carer
- the approximate number of children you have cared for
- training
- your experience of specialist fostering schemes
- relevant work experience.

The placement

Inform the court of:

- date(s) when the child was placed with you
- where the child came from (own home, from another placement, from hospital etc.)
- the circumstances of the child's arrival and a factual description of the child (including marks, bruises or apparent illnesses)
- if the child is no longer with the you, the circumstances in which he/ she left.

The child

Before giving your opinion about any specific concerns, try to describe factually the child's:

- eating
- sleeping
- toileting
- hygiene
- health
- speech
- play
- development
- behaviour.

Describe any aspects of the child which have changed during the placement. (Refer to the age-related Assessment and Action Records. These form part of the Department of Health system *Looking after Children* which is being implemented in a phased programme across local authorities.)

Consider the impact on the child of visits from the social worker or other professionals.

School

Have arrangements for school or transportation changed and if so, how? What has been the impact on the child of any change?

Contact issues

'Contact' includes phone calls and letters between the child and family, not just visits. Distinguish a factual description of, for example, the child's behaviour before and after contact from your opinion about the impact of contact on the child. Describe:

- the circumstances of the child's contact with parents, brothers and sisters, other relatives and friends
- contact on significant events such as birthdays and religious holidays
- your involvement with child's family, if any.

Children's experience of contact visits

> **Children are likely to manifest distress or difficult behaviour before, during and after contact sessions. In describing such behaviour to the court, it is important to be objective and to take account of possible different reasons for such behaviour.**

What the child said

When reporting what the child has said, explain the surrounding circumstances including the setting and what happened to prompt the child's comments. Were they spontaneous? Give dates if possible; explain whether you made a note of the conversation and if so, how soon after it took place. Consider what the child said in relation to:

- life at home
- court proceedings
- self-esteem
- relationships
- the future.